MOSTLY MISCHIEF

H. W. TILMAN

Still, I think the immense act has something about it human and excusable; and when I endeavour to analyse the reason of this feeling I find it to lie, not in the fact that the thing was big or bold or successful, but in the fact that the thing was perfectly useless to everybody, including the person who did it.

G. K. CHESTERTON

Surtsey and the new volcanic island, 1965

MOSTLY MISCHIEF

H. W. TILMAN

TILMAN

First published 1966 by Hollis & Carter Ltd
This edition published 2016 by Tilman Books
www.tilmanbooks.com
a joint venture by
Lodestar Books www.lodestarbooks.com
and Vertebrate Publishing www.v-publishing.co.uk

Cover design by Jane Beagley
Vertebrate Graphics Ltd. www.v-graphics.co.uk

Lodestar Books has asserted their right
to be identified as the Editor of this Work

Series editor Dick Wynne
Series researcher Bob Comlay

The publisher has made reasonable effort to locate
the holders of copyright in the illustrations in this book,
and will be pleased to hear from them regarding
correct attribution in future editions

Typeset in Baskerville from Storm Type Foundry
Printed and bound by Pulsio, Bulgaria
All papers used by Tilman Books are sourced responsibly

The author gratefully acknowledges permission to quote from the following publications: from Hillaire Belloc's *The Cruise of the Nona*, by courtesy of Messrs. Constable; from *The Arctic Pilot*, Volumes II and III, and from an Admiralty *Notice to Mariners*, by courtesy of H. M. Stationery Office; from *The Pilot of Arctic Canada, 1960*, by courtesy of the Domnion Hydrographer, Marine Sciences Branch, Department of Mines and Technical Surveys; from an *American Pilot Chart*, by courtesy of the U.S. Naval Oceanographic Office; from an article by Dr D. C. Blanchard in *Oceanus*, by courtesy of Woods Hole Oceanographic Institution; and from Lecky's *Wrinkles in Practical Navigation*, by courtesy of Messrs. George Philip.

Contents

Photographs

Maps

Foreword

Roger D. Taylor

I'VE JUST FINISHED READING H. W. Tilman's eight sailing and mountaineering books for... I don't know... maybe the twentieth time. Reading Tilman is a continuous work-in-progress, rather like painting the Forth Bridge. Finish the last page and you're just about ready to start all over again. Throw in too the seven pure mountaineering books and you have several life-times' worth of undiminished reading pleasure. Tilman's books are the nearest I get to having a permanent bedside companion. They're never far away. Sometimes I read them cover to cover, other times I browse and dip. Tilman is endlessly fascinating, and infuriating too. His adventures serve as both inspiration and warning. He is a guiding light and a hero, yet riddled with flaws and contradictions.

Let's be more specific. Tilman came to sailing late—in his mid-fifties—and it shows. Although he became a good ocean navigator, taking his pilot cutters through dangerous and difficult waters, he didn't, I suspect, ever achieve the fluency and sureness in close-quarter boat handling that only a lifetime of sailing can develop. For sure he was sailing unhandy boats, often with novice crews, but over the years he produced a litany of bumps, scrapes and near misses at moorings and jetties from Angmagssalik to Punta Arenas. To his credit he is brutally honest about this and the first to lampoon his own errors.

The more I read Tilman, the more I am convinced that his attitude to the proximity of land was not as well-honed or cautious as it should have been. His boats were neither the quickest nor the most close-winded, nor were their engines particularly reliable, yet time and again he stands in close, often, it seems, just for the hell of it. He talks of the *Arctic Pilot*'s warning of the race off Langanes in northeast Iceland, then sails past it 'a quarter of a mile off'. Time and again he takes short cuts through dodgy passages. Going aground is a regular pastime.

In one sense much of this was inevitable. Tilman was not just going sailing. He was going sailing in order to go climbing, therefore he had to get in close and find suitable anchorages from which the climbers could strike out. The sailing was only ever a means to an end. Nevertheless, the safety of the ship was still paramount and on that score he had some significant lapses.

The grounding that eventually led to the loss of his first pilot cutter, his beloved *Mischief*, was the result of curiously inattentive seamanship. Becalmed at night, in fog, off the southern tip of Jan Mayen, where he already knew there were off-lying rocks and a strong northerly set, he turned in and left the deck to a complete novice, with no instructions. Fifteen or twenty minutes' motoring due east would probably have been enough to take *Mischief* out of potential danger.

His next pilot cutter, *Sea Breeze*, was lost on the East Greenland coast when a combination of engine failure and lack of wind put the boat completely at the mercy of ice floes, which pushed her onto a rocky islet. The crew was lucky to be able to scramble onto a nearby ledge. Had *Sea Breeze* been equipped with a pair of sweeps, as was his next cutter, the loss may have been averted. Given that Tilman's northern voyages were largely aimed at penetrating ice fields in order to reach remote anchorages, and given the general unreliability of his engines, and his awareness that to be without any motive power when amongst ice floes was extremely dangerous, it is again curious that it took him so long to equip himself with sweeps.

Tilman's third and final pilot cutter, *Baroque*, survived, but only just. Whilst off north-east Spitsbergen he sailed her almost inadvertently between two islands, grounding her firmly on the interconnecting reef, a lapse he put down to tiredness. Only heroic and seamanlike action—the throwing overboard of tons of pig-iron ballast, followed by nail-biting fun-and-games laying out anchors and trying to winch her off—saved her. Tilman and his crew re-ballasted her with rocks from a remote beach and successfully sailed her back home. Poor old *Baroque* had to go through the mill once again. Leaving harbour in East Greenland, and wrongly assuming that the steep shore meant he could go in close, Tilman again ran her aground, on the ebb. Despite masthead lines to the shore she dried out the wrong way and subsequently filled on the incoming tide. He was lucky that help was at hand to pump her out and refloat her, and to fix the engine.

Tilman was always ready with an apposite quote and one of his favourites was from the Prussian General von Moltke: 'Few plans can withstand contact with the enemy'. I often think he may have done well to paraphrase it: 'Few boats can withstand contact with land'.

Tilman's uncompromising ambitions locked him into a kind of vicious circle. The ultimate aim of his voyages was to climb. However his boat had to be looked after while the climbers were away. He therefore needed a biggish crew and a boat large enough to carry them and their equipment and stores. Although a man of some means—his father had been a wealthy Liverpool sugar merchant—he was frugal by nature, and solved the boat problem by using Bristol Channel pilot cutters, craft well past their useful life and relatively cheap to buy.

He was therefore in a position where he was constantly scouring docksides for crew who, once found and shipped aboard, were often unhappy with the spartan conditions and the constant pumping that attended all his voyages. Occasionally his famously terse adverts in *The Times*, typically offering 'no pay, no prospects, not much pleasure', yielded some gems, but most of his voyages were beset by crew problems of one sort or another, some verging on the mutinous. The result of all this was that much of his time and energy at sea was taken up with a monumental struggle to keep his craft afloat and his crew on board. As Tilman often lamented, with the right crew—and he did from time to time hit on an excellent combination—anything was possible, but an unwilling crew usually led to an unsuccessful voyage. He did not exclude himself from blame on this point. As an ex-soldier he was well aware of the military maxim that there are no bad armies, only bad officers.

In a sense his achievements are all the greater for his persistence in the face of constant setbacks: broken spars, blown-out sails, sprung planks, deserting crew and so on. He was no youngster either, when coping with all of this. Perhaps that's one of my favourite aspects of his tales: his indomitable, bloody-minded refusal to give up. But more than that, I come back again and again for the pure quality of his writing—witty, erudite, understated, self-deprecating. There was a lot more to him than the allegedly misogynistic old curmudgeon of popular portrayal. He was a complex man and a deep thinker. Even in the moments of greatest despair, as everything goes wrong for him, one senses that he is looking at it all with a twinkle in his eye. He was a subaltern in the First World War trenches at the age of seventeen and saw most of his comrades killed. Perhaps that is what led him never to take himself, or his subsequent life, too seriously. Perhaps too that is what gave him his sometimes cavalier approach to his own safety, both in the mountains and at sea. It certainly gave him a kind of detached and often well-camouflaged wisdom which only regular re-reading can fully uncover.

Roger D. Taylor
September 2015

PART ONE

Bylot Island, Baffin Bay
Mischief

May–September, 1963

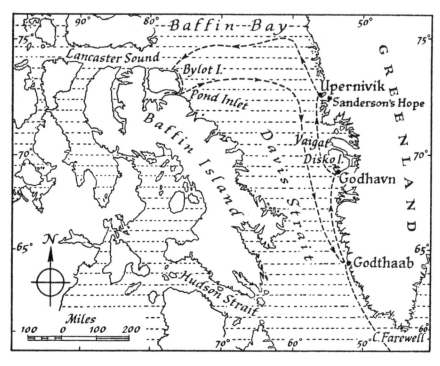

Map 1: Bylot Island, Baffin Bay, 1963

CHAPTER I

PLANS AND PREPARATIONS

AS THE TEXAN OIL-MAN PUT IT: 'When you strike oil, stop boring.' After two voyages to Davis Strait and the adjacent coasts of West Greenland and Baffin Island I felt that I had also, as it were, struck oil, having found a cruising ground that fulfilled all expectations. In a region to which the voyage is not too long, Arctic waters beat upon coasts that are wild and little frequented and that are studded with unclimbed mountains. Here in summer one enjoys more or less continuous daylight, the pale skies and soft colours of the north, and above all the romance and excitement of icebergs and pack-ice seen at close quarters from the deck of a small boat. When sailing, perhaps, in fog, a little uncertain of one's position, listening to the menacing growl of pack-ice, it is easy to imagine oneself in company with John Davis aboard his 50-ton ship *Mooneshine*, or with any of those hardy spirits, the Elizabethan sailor-explorers in search of a north-west passage. As Belloc wrote of the amateur sailor: 'In venturing in sail upon strange coasts we are seeking those first experiences, and trying to feel as felt the earlier man in a happier time, to see the world as they saw it.'

The west coast of Greenland from Cape Farewell to Cape York (which can be regarded as almost beyond the northernmost limit for a small boat) is 900 miles long, for the most part fronted with uninhabited islands, islets, and skerries, and indented with long, fascinating fjords generously blessed with mountains and glaciers. On the opposite side of Davis Strait the east coast of Baffin Island is not much shorter and has likewise its islands, fjords, and mountains, though these are rather too rounded and lacking in true Alpine character to attract the mountaineer. But from the amateur explorer's point of view this coast has the advantage over Greenland of having no ports or towns, very few Eskimo settlements, and maps that are pleasingly vague. Compared with the Greenland coast it is frighteningly barren and the climate is cooler and cloudier. The cause of these conditions is the cold, south-going Canadian, or Labrador, current bringing bergs and pack-ice down from Baffin Bay and the great ice-filled sounds leading to it—Smith, Jones, and Lancaster Sounds. On this account, too, except for a brief period in August and September, the Canadian coast is heavily beset with ice. The West Greenland coast, on the other hand, is washed by a north-going current bringing comparatively warm water from the Atlantic, and although the immense Greenland glaciers are the source of nearly all the icebergs met with on either coast, this west coast is in summer more or less free from pack-ice.

In so vast a field, with so many attractive fjords and their attendant mountains asking to be visited, the choice of an objective is difficult; and a voyage in my opinion should have some objective beyond that of crossing an ocean or making a passage. Naturally the amateur sailor derives much satisfaction from hitting off the continent or country at which he is aiming, but nowadays this modest ambition is achieved more often than not and the successful voyager, having bought a few souvenirs to support his claim, has nothing to do but come back:

> Nothing to sing but songs,
> Ah well, alas, and alack,
> Nowhere to go but out
> Nowhere to come but back.

After studying the *Arctic Pilot* I picked upon Bylot Island as a likely objective for 1963. It lies off the north-east corner of Baffin Island separated from it by the ten-mile wide Pond Inlet. It is in Lat. 73°N., further north than *Mischief* had been before and as far north as she is likely to get in those regions. To find ice-free water further north than this one would have to go to Spitsbergen where in favourable seasons one might reach Lat. 78°N. without even seeing ice. Thus even the reaching of Bylot Island was a challenge. There was no certainty that it could be reached, that the ice would have cleared away or be sufficiently open for a small, unstrengthened vessel like *Mischief* to navigate. According to the ice-charts there seemed little doubt that by the end of August and throughout September the sea up there would be navigable. So if the worst came to the worst we could wait. But that would mean a late homeward voyage across the Atlantic in October which the prudent yachtsman would wish to avoid. In the Atlantic in October the percentage of gales shows a marked increase.

The island is named after Robert Bylot who acted as mate to Hudson on his fourth voyage in *Discovery* in 1610. This was the ill-fated voyage when, as the result of a mutiny, Hudson himself, his son John, and seven seamen were turned adrift in an open boat 'without food, drink, fire, clothing, or other necessaries' in the great unexplored Bay to fend for themselves, or in other words to die. Bylot himself took no leading part in the mutiny but the fact that he escaped being put over the side seems to show that he was no very ardent supporter of his captain, Henry Hudson. Perhaps the mutineers had need of his skill, for he was then put in charge of the ship. Before they had won clear of Hudson's Strait four of the leading mutineers had been killed by Eskimos and *Discovery* finally struggled into Bantry Bay on September 6th, 1611, with only nine survivors, all in a state of starvation. The survivors were in a position to give their account of events without fear of contradiction, and although an enquiry was held nothing came of it and no one was brought to book. Bylot's services were evidently of value for he went on to make two more voyages both in the same ship, *Discovery*, of only fifty-five tons. The first was with Baffin in 1615 when they again explored Hudson Bay, when Baffin gave it as his considered opinion that no north-west passage would be found in that direction and that Davis Strait offered the only hope. Consequently in 1616 they sailed again, with Bylot as master and Baffin as pilot, when *Discovery* reached Lat. 77° 45′ N. On this outstanding voyage Baffin Bay, and Smith, Jones, and Lancaster Sounds were discovered and named. No advance of importance towards the discovery of a north-west passage was to be made for the next two hundred years.

In my view, distorted though it may be, Bylot Island had much in its favour, being difficult to reach, little known, uninhabited, and mountainous. In 1939 P. D. Baird, a well known Arctic traveller, had made a single-handed sledge journey with dogs inland from the Pond Inlet coast. Owing to soft snow on the north-flowing glaciers he did not get through to the north coast. In May 1954 a party of American scientists landed by air on the ice in Pond Inlet and spent a month on the island at a base on the south coast. They had climbed two mountains close inland from there, the 5800-foot Mt Thule, and another of about 6000 feet. A general account of this appears in a book called *Spring on an Arctic Island* by Katharine Scherman, the wife of one of the scientists.

With so little background knowledge I had doubts as to whether the mountains would be of much interest. It seemed probable that they would be like those at the tip of the Cumberland Peninsula which we had climbed the previous year and their description in the *Arctic Pilot*—a 1947 edition—confirmed this: 'Bylot Island is formed of crystalline rocks and in physical character closely resembles the adjacent north-east part of Baffin Island. The general elevation of the interior ranges from 2000 feet to 3000 feet and the coastal highlands are covered with an ice cap which extends 10 to 15 miles inland, the interior, according to the Eskimos, being free of snow during summer. The ice-rim feeds numerous glaciers, some of which discharge bergs.'

This 1947 account is evidently largely guesswork and wrong in several respects; the general elevation is from 3000 feet to 6000 feet and the ice cap covers most of the elevated interior which in summer is by no means free from snow. The 1960 edition of the Canadian publication *Pilot of Arctic Canada*, up to date and more accurate, made the mountains, too, sound quite impressive: 'The second largest ice-field (second to the Penny ice cap on Baffin Island) occupies the greater part of Bylot Island and is only slightly lower than the Penny ice cap, mountain peaks rising through it to attain altitudes of over 6000 feet … On the south coast the Castle Gables, an Alpine-like mountain rising to 4850 feet with serrated ridges and three major, jagged crests, is a prominent summit between Kaparoqtalik and Sermilik glaciers. Mt Thule, about 5800 feet high, stands about five miles north-westward of Sermilik glacier.' This sounded like the real thing but on some air photographs, which I received from a friend in the Canadian Survey, Castle Gables appeared as a ridge of rotten rock devoid of ice or snow, and Mt Thule a rounded summit little higher than the surrounding snow-field.

No mountains are to be despised. At my time of life, especially, one's attitude towards any mountain can hardly be too humble. I had, however, to consider the young, ardent climber whom, I hoped, might be persuaded to accompany me. I could hardly ask him to suffer a four-month voyage for the sake of climbing mountains like Castle

Gables or Thule. A more worthwhile challenge would be a crossing of the island. It is about sixty miles from north to south, for the most part glaciers and snow-fields. The whole island, by the way, covers some 4000 square miles—small enough compared with the 200,000 square miles of Baffin Island which is roughly two-and-one-half times the size of the British Isles. If we succeeded it would be the first complete crossing. Much virtue in being the first. To a mountaineer a first ascent is the great prize. In the nature of things there are nowadays, in the more accessible mountainous regions, few first ascents left to be made. Aspirants for mountaineering fame are thus driven to making first ascents by all the remaining possible and impossible routes on an ascending scale of difficulty and danger, first ascents in winter, first ascents by moonlight or by no light at all, and so on, some spurred by dedication to the craft, some perhaps seeking the bubble reputation even in the cannon's mouth.

Mischief has been fully described before. She is a Bristol Channel pilot cutter built at Cardiff in 1906 of 29 tons T.M., 45 feet long, 13 feet beam, drawing 7 feet 6 inches aft. Apart from a 40-h.p. Perkins diesel auxiliary engine, winches for the staysail sheets and the main halyard, and a wire guard-rail, she is not much changed from when she was a working boat—the same heavy gear and rigging, heavy canvas sails, and accommodation below that might be described as simple. The winches and the guard-rail make her easier and safer to handle, the engine allows for some indifferent seamanship on the part of the skipper and is in any case essential among ice floes and in the windless Greenland fjords if one wants to cover any ground. Moreover, instead of the two men or man and boy who used to work her in and out of the Bristol Channel, the crew now generally comprises five or six so that they are, comparatively speaking, in clover. On the other hand in her working days she did not cross oceans or spend weeks or months at sea.

The crew began to assemble at Lymington about May 13th, allowing a full week to get the spars and running rigging set up, the sails bent, and stores stowed. This was as well because the weather proved wet and unfavourable for work and at the last moment we found signs of rot in the knightheads, the vertical stem timbers either side of the bowsprit. These had to be replaced together with a new breast-hook, the timber which holds together the bows. In an old boat rot or soft spots in the timbers is endemic and generally to be found if persistently sought. It is a case of the more you stir the more it stinks. One cannot afford to be too fussy. A boat must be ripe indeed if without any cautionary hints and warnings she opens up like a basket. Apart from when she is occasionally called on to shunt ice *Mischief* is handled with the tender care due to one of her age. We avoid, if possible, prolonged bashing into head seas. If she begins to tremble with excitement, as she sometimes does when doing over six knots, I take it as a hint to reduce sail. In the open sea one can steer a point or even two points off the required course if it will make the motion easier, and since the average helmsman is likely to be that much off course anyway it makes no difference in the long run. Or one can heave to for the sake of peace and quiet, especially if the cook is having trouble in the galley and the evening meal is in jeopardy.

The crews for *Mischief*'s nine voyages have all been more or less inexperienced. Most sailing men either have their own boats to sail or are engaged to crew for friends, while the few who have the opportunity to make a long cruise prefer to go in search of sun and warmth. In 1963 I had what was probably the least experienced crew of any. With one exception I doubt if any of them had been to sea before in a small boat. However the exception had enough experience to make up the deficiency of the rest. Ed Mikeska was a professional seaman who had sailed in all kinds of ships from large yachts to ice-breakers. In fact his last spell at sea had been in a Canadian ice-breaker in the Canadian Arctic. He was a Pole, in his 'teens when the Germans invaded Poland, who had got away to England and served in the war at sea with the Free Poles. I had corresponded with him off and on for some time and he had been on the point of coming with me on an earlier voyage to the Southern Ocean but had thought better of it. This time, since his mind seemed fully made up, I took him on and felt I was lucky to have on board such a thorough seaman. By the time one has got clear of the English Channel and its perilous shipping lanes even a green crew should have shaken down, got over their seasickness, and be on the way to becoming useful, but those first two or three days in the Channel can be very wearing for the skipper unless backed by an experienced hand like Ed Mikeska. Though it may have been for the good of their souls his hazing of the crew was perhaps too much like that of a bucko mate.

Ed took the keenest interest in boats and in all aspects of the sea and was knowledgeable about most of them. On joining he had some disparaging remarks to make about *Mischief*, in fact in his view she seemed scarcely seaworthy—the cockpit was big enough to constitute a death-trap, the companionway facing aft would merely conduct half the ocean into the cabin, and the skylight was another vulnerable point that endangered the ship. The rigging of her, too, could in several ways be improved. A man's most cherished possession be it a woman or a ship, a horse or a favourite dog, is seldom without blemishes, and though the man himself may be aware of them he does not really enjoy having them brought to his notice. I had to remind Ed of the remark of the skipper of a coasting brig to his newly-joined mate: 'What I want from you Mr Mate is silence, and not too much of that.'

Then there was Mike Taylor, young and strong, so reluctant to settle down in the Channel Islands as an estate agent in his father's office that he had been working as a labourer in the Berthon Boatyard. I'm afraid the voyage unsettled him still more; I had a brief meeting with him recently in Sydney where he had just arrived.

Bruce Reid, also young, had left St Andrews University (with which I have a sort of back-door relationship), unfortunately without a degree, his climbing activities having precluded his devoting much time to the study of history. He had since settled for the R.A.F. but would not be needed until October. Stephen Pitt, the youngest of all, after leaving school at Malvern had worked in a London office in the timber business without acquiring any great love for it. His parents were a little concerned at his wanting to go to sea in *Mischief* and since they lived within easy reach of Lymington I soon learnt how they thought about it. Unable to be like the deaf adder that stoppeth her ears I soon began to feel all the guilt and none of the pleasure of a successful seducer of youth.

All these had been enlisted voluntarily and almost painlessly without any advertising or having to scratch around and solicit. None of them, however, had shown any willingness to take on the job of cook, the most important in the ship. My last victim, Bob Sargent, who lived in Edinburgh, I got hold of in a more devious way. My friend Dr David

Lewis, in search of crew for a maiden voyage to northern waters in his catamaran Rehu Moana, had by no means eschewed publicity and had, in consequence, received a host of applicants. Among those rejects whom he passed on to me was young Bob Sargent. Luckily I had occasion to go north to St Andrews and we arranged to meet for breakfast at Princes Street station in Edinburgh. He was then studying in a business college of the House of Fraser, found it singularly unrefreshing, and was hell-bent on going on some expedition, no matter where. He had never been to sea and had no other useful experience or skills to offer but he said he could cook. Cooking for oneself on a gas or electric stove in a house that seldom rocks is quite different to cooking for six men on a Primus stove at sea in *Mischief*'s galley, a galley, by the way, which is sited forward of the mast in the most lively part of the ship. After I had explained and even stressed all these differences to Bob his confidence remained unshaken. So I agreed to take him as cook, a gamble that happened to come off.

CHAPTER II

TO GODTHAAB

H OWEVER MANY TIMES IT HAS BEEN DONE, the act of casting off the warps and letting go one's last hold of the shore at the start of a voyage has about it something solemn and irrevocable, like marriage, for better or for worse. True, one is not afloat for a lifetime, but when mewed up with five fellow humans for four months, should one or two of them prove to be misfits, it might well seem like a lifetime. One feels uneasy, too, that something vital may have been forgotten, like the proverbial Dutchman who left behind his anchor. To put back would make one feel too much of a fool, while to put in at any other home port after the ship had been cleared for a foreign port would lead H.M. Customs to suspect some hanky-panky. And there is the fear that things may go wrong in front of the crowd of friends, or even admirers, who have gathered on the quay to wave farewell; such as on a memorable occasion at Punta Arenas when we went aground hard and fast within spitting distance of the crowd of admirers on the quay we had just left; or more recently at Albany in Australia when, upon hoisting the staysail to blow the ship's head clear of the jetty, the block strop broke and the sail collapsed on the heads of the chaps hoisting it.

No untimely mishaps occurred when we cast off on the morning of May 23rd. In consideration of *Mischief*'s draft and the crowded river, the Harbour Master's launch was in attendance to see us away. In the Solent we hoisted sail. The wind being foul, we had to tack four times before reaching the Needles, thus giving the crew a little sail drill. Outside, the wind obliged by veering more northerly just as if to spite the meteorological boys who had forecast it backing to south-west. We could not have been treated more kindly, the glass remained high and the sea calm. No one was seasick and during the night no steamers menaced us. My personal bliss was only slightly marred by some very queer results from sun sights which put us ashore in West Bay. One's navigation, like everything else about a ship, must be kept in good repair and free from rust.

Our progress down Channel was stately and slow. On the 24th we were still off Start Point and did not sight the Lizard until late that evening, the weather hazy with light easterly winds. Meantime, in these cosmopolitan waters, a Russian sail-training ship passed us under engine, a Dutch submarine was sighted, and a French trawler shot by so close under our stern that we had to haul in the log-line. I thought this friendly of them but unnecessary. Early on the 26th we found ourselves becalmed near the Seven Stones light-vessel with the tide setting us briskly towards the rocks and the white breaking water two miles to the south-west. We had to start the engine to get clear. Formerly the engine used not to start with the promptitude that one would wish, so now we carried ether and whenever the engine was required administered a whiff with gratifying effect. In the march of science I'm afraid I lag far behind and would never myself have suspected that ether would have such a galvanizing effect upon diesel engines.

That evening we had some wind and for my part a restless night. In spite of their gentle initiation the crew were still pretty inept, hazy about which rope to pull or even how to manage the pumps and stopcocks on the lavatory. A reported alarming leak was the result of someone having failed to turn off the lavatory inflow, and no sooner had this been put right when Stephen reported 'water pouring in at the bow'. This proved to be some damp round the new breast-hook. But Ed remained uneasy and while searching the ship for leaks promised us a gale by morning. We did in fact put in a reef at 3 a.m. but the morning broke fine and sunny with a moderately rough sea. This pleased the crew who were beginning to think sailing a dull, slow business. Bob proved his worth by producing breakfast as usual and for supper bangers and mash with fried onions. By noon we had logged over 100 miles for the twenty-four hours. We at last felt we were getting somewhere for we were then eighty miles south-west of the Fastnet.

The last four days of May gave us all that could be wished for in the way of weather. With a steady beam wind at north-east we had hardly to touch a sheet. Leaving the genoa up all night, we recorded runs of 90, 95, 131, and 121 miles. Ever since leaving we had had trouble with the charging engine on which the battery and hence the cabin lights, the binnacle light, and the use of the wireless receiver depended. For the time we had to forego weather reports and, more important, time signals. Besides keeping a Supplementary Ship's Log for the Meteorological Office, Ed doubled the role of mate and engineer. As a matter of routine he spent an hour each day wrestling with the charging engine, the session ending invariably in failure and abuse both in English and Polish. Having found an old sparking plug that looked as if it should have long since been thrown overboard I gave it Ed to try. Whereupon the engine started without a murmur. This much relieved Ed who, for the next few days, until we were out of range, could listen to the weather forecasts to which he was so much addicted. Though we may all like to have our fortunes told few of us are weak-minded enough to believe what we are told. Similarly I think it a mistake to rely for one's peace of mind upon forecasts of fair weather or to become unduly worried by forecasts of foul weather. As Dr Johnson remarks: 'Let us cease to consider what may never happen, and what, when it shall happen, will laugh at human speculation.' When far from land the weather must be taken as it comes and fortunately bad weather seldom springs upon one without warning, leaving no time to shorten sail. If it behaved like that one would want not forecasts but a running commentary.

Perhaps it was presumptuous of me at this early stage to bake a cake. It got away to a bad start, rising very slowly, accompanied, as I noticed, by a rising wind. Before the cake was done we had reefed both main and staysail and a little later we hove to, the wind being from ahead. Sailing hard into it made us leak a bit round the stemhead. The *Clarkenden*, bound west, closed and spoke to us by loud-hailer, offering to report us at Lloyd's. On the following day we let draw and made some westing but the wind soon increased to Force 7 and again we hove to. In rough weather, do what one may, *Mischief*'s skylight is never watertight. We can ship a canvas cover and sit below in the gloom of an aquarium and only a little less wet. Even with the cover shipped, when a sea comes on deck those on the lee side of the cabin get a shower-bath. Matters below were not mended when the teapot upset, scalding Mike's hand and arm. Bob took his watch that night.

In summer in the Atlantic a blow rarely lasts for more than twenty-four hours. By next day, having straightened things up below and on deck, we were under all plain sail with a good quartering wind. But the sky remained obstinately overcast and three days went by before I got a sight, a sight which put us thirty miles south of our dead reckoning position. When hove to, *Mischief* makes about one knot crabwise, which is fair enough provided one has plenty of sea-room. I have since had a brief experience with a parachute anchor and think it might hold a boat even as heavy as *Mischief*. To save that amount of drift would be a useful achievement.

By June 4th we had done our first thousand miles. On the 7th, when about 500 miles from Cape Farewell, we suffered a flat calm from 6 a.m. until midnight. We launched our nine-foot dinghy in order to take pictures of *Mischief* with her sails hanging limp and of the Atlantic in a most benign mood. We ran the engine for an hour to exercise it and in order to appreciate more fully the profound silence when it stopped. As we waited patiently for a wind Ed, our meteorological expert, began to speak of calms that had lasted for six weeks. In view of their recent history the Poles, as a nation, have a right to suspect the worst from their fellow men or at any rate from those who are their immediate neighbours, but Ed Mikeska's suspicions embraced also the weather. Few of the well-known signs that are supposed to promise fair weather found any favour in his eyes while any signs of ill-omen were given full value and filled him with apprehensive gloom. We had some wind that night and when the dawn broke luridly red the prospect of six weeks' calm had to yield place to that of an imminent gale.

In the end we had a fine easterly breeze which gave us a lift of sixty-five miles in twelve hours. This proved to be the last log reading we were to take for some time, the rotator on the log having been bitten off by some marine monster. It is of course satisfactory to be able to read off from hour to hour the distance covered and what speed one is doing, but a sufficiently accurate estimate can be made by the helmsman who at the end of his watch logs his idea of the distance run. One man will underestimate and another will overestimate and at the end of the day the total will not be far out. This, together with the course steered, enables the navigator to plot the assumed position which sooner or later he will be able to check by sights. The easterly wind brought with it thick, drizzly weather, the air temperature dropping to 45° and the sea to 43°. On this I abandoned my early-morning ritual of pouring over my head three buckets of sea water, and I gave it up more readily because there was no one with whom to compete in this endurance test. On former voyages, as the sea temperature gradually dropped, some of us have vied with each other as to who would or could longest maintain this shocking habit.

In the prevailing thick weather Ed hastened to hoist an umbrella-like radar reflector which, with seamanlike prudence, he had brought with him. The theory is that a wooden vessel does not show up on a radar screen and most yachtsmen carry various kinds of metal devices in the hope that their presence will thus be made obvious to an oncoming steamer. An expert has recently told me that *Mischief*'s massive wire shrouds should act as well or better than any reflector. Perhaps hoisting radar reflectors is merely an act of faith, just as not many years ago Europeans in the tropics used to wear sun helmets. Sitting under the protection of Ed's umbrella I can't say that I felt any more secure, nor would it do to relax one's vigilance on this account. In any case the waters we were then sailing are so unfrequented by ships that only if I had shipped an entire crew of Jonahs were we likely to be hit by one. We ourselves stood far more chance of hitting an iceberg for we were only some 200 miles east of Cape Farewell. Homeward bound round Cape Farewell in 1962 we had sighted an iceberg 140 miles south-east of it.

These icebergs off Cape Farewell and the vicinity originate in the glaciers of the east coast of Greenland. Owing to the inaccessibility of the northern parts of this coast, information about the iceberg-discharging glaciers and their productivity is less complete than for the west coast where the average annual discharge of bergs from all the bigger glaciers is pretty well known. The annual discharge is thought to be about equal for both coasts, but the east coast bergs do not reach the sea so quickly and in many cases are held up by the pack-ice near their sources. Moreover a large number never leave the fjords into which they are calved owing to the shallowness of the water at the fjord entrance. In Scoresby Sund, for example, in Lat. 70° N. the majority of icebergs never leave the fjord. The most productive glaciers are all south of Lat. 68°. The main flow of bergs round Cape Farewell takes place from April to August; off there several hundred have been reported in sight from a ship at one time. In autumn the number decreases rapidly and in winter Cape Farewell is more or less free from bergs.

The only safeguard against icebergs is vigilance and it was partly on their account that on June 12th we spent an uneasy night. With the glass falling steeply, accompanied by heavy rain, the wind increased until it was gusting to about Force 8. We were running fast under twin staysails and in order to reduce speed we dropped one of them. With no visibility at all to speak of we were still going too fast. I was in two minds about having the starboard sail down when the matter was settled for me by its sheet parting. In spite of its violent flogging we got the sail in undamaged. At dawn the wind eased and the sun came out, the prelude to a lovely day, but it had been no fun sailing thus unsighted, and uncertain whether or no there were any icebergs about. The fact that so far none had been sighted did not, of course, carry complete assurance.

On June 14th, a cold, grey day, when we were about fifty miles south of Cape Farewell we began steering north to close the land in order to benefit by the current which sweeps round the cape and up the west coast. Sights showed that we had already had a lift of twenty miles from the current. Early next day we sighted pack-ice ahead and to starboard but still no bergs. The wind obliged us to make long boards and each time we came inshore we met loose floes on the edge of the pack. I had expected to find better weather west of the cape but for the next three days we had dull, lowering skies and bitter head winds, the air temperature falling to 39° and then to 34°. The sea temperature remained at 37°. At last we began meeting icebergs though they were remarkably few compared with the previous summer. In the prevailing dull weather the nights were not as light as they should have been and for two hours either side of midnight, when visibility became pretty poor, we usually hove to.

So far we had had a good passage. We had rounded Cape Farewell in twenty-three days, the same time as in 1962, whereas in 1961 it had cost us thirty-five days. Easterly winds at the start had given us a good push and by keeping well north we had perhaps avoided some of the westerly winds. On the 17th we were in Lat. 61° 16′ and that afternoon when the weather cleared we closed the land north of Arsuk

Fjord where there is a cryolite mine. We watched a small cargo vessel work her way in there through scattered floes. Cryolite is used in the manufacture of aluminium and in the enamelling of iron; according to the *Arctic Pilot* 20,000 tons are exported from there annually. By now icebergs had become a normal feature of the seascape; trawlers too, for we were now on the first of the fishing banks, rich in cod and halibut, which extend well up the West Greenland coast. That summer an international body was engaged in fishery research in these waters and on behalf of this Ed Mikeska had undertaken the making of plankton hauls close inshore. We made our first haul that evening. The sample in its glass jar resembled in colour and consistency a weak brew of tomato soup. Hauling in the fine mesh net at the end of some twenty fathoms of rope required two men.

My expectation of pleasant June weather in Davis Strait, based on previous experience, at last began to be realised. On a warm, sunny afternoon the magic of a northern summer day had us in thrall as we sailed silently over a placid, pale blue sea dotted with bergs, while inland the dark outline of the coastal mountains was split by the broad, glistening ice-stream of the ten-mile wide Frederikshaab Glacier. The day before, the 'blink' from this great mass of ice had been visible in the sky. We sailed close past the Portuguese three-masted schooner *Antonio Domino* at anchor, with her fleet of fifty or sixty dories scattered over the surrounding sea. A dog barked at us and the voices of two men talking on deck were carried to us over the quiet water long after we had passed.

Early on June 21st we sighted the cluster of islets at the entrance to the Godthaab Fjord and in the distance the two peaks known as the Beacons of Godthaab—Sermilsiak, nearly 4000 feet high which is shaped like a saddle with a high pommel, and Hjortataken to the south like a high pillar. Though the entrance between the islets and a reef to the north of them is narrow, on a clear day there is no difficulty, and thereafter the fjord is wide and free from dangers for twelve miles up to the narrow harbour entrance. John Davis anchored here in 1585—he called it Gilbert Sound—and had friendly exchanges with the Eskimos. I was immediately struck by the amount of snow still lying low on the surrounding hills and even on islands right down to the water's edge. From this, infected perhaps by Ed's pessimism, I began drawing gloomy conclusions about the lateness of the season and the small chance of finding ice-free water in Baffin Bay.

Arrived in the small land-locked harbour with its dog-leg entrance we anchored in our usual berth with the quay half a cable away on one side and on the other, only some twenty yards away, a thirty-foot wall of rock. This wall is decorated, or desecrated, with the names of various visiting ships painted in large white letters. Before we left, Stephen, not to be outdone in vandalism, added *Mischief*'s name to the record. *Mallemuken*, a small Danish naval vessel used mainly for fishery protection, was moored in her usual berth close to us. Almost every time we had visited Godthaab she had been there and we had usually managed to make use of her hot shower bath. We had not to wait before going ashore. At Godthaab there are no formalities for visiting yachts, possibly because, other than *Mischief*, there are not any. Ashore we made a useful friend in Bond Elliot, a Canadian, agent for the Canadian firm that ran the Catalina seaplanes which carry mail and passengers between the various ports on the West Greenland coast. He found for us a solenoid starter for our Perkins engine which had burnt out and had made for us in their workshop a new petrol tank for the Stuart Turner charging engine. He also did his best to obtain an ice report for Baffin Bay but without success. Owing to the amount of snow still about it was undoubtedly much colder ashore than it had been in previous summers. Thanks to the cold there were no clouds of mosquitoes to plague us. In former summers it had been common to see men working in the open with nets over their heads.

The weather was also wetter and windier than usual; in fact we might as well have been in England. On the night of our arrival a heavy southerly gale set in with torrential rain. Three trawlers and the survey vessel *Dana* came in for shelter. Next day, the gale continuing, we stayed on board and set an anchor watch, for we were horribly close to the rock wall. The dinghy, inadequately secured, went adrift and no one saw it go. We expected to find it broken up, as we deserved, on the rocks at the shallow end of the harbour, and by great luck an R.C. padre returning in his motor boat from a parochial visit up the fjord spotted it there. Taking two of the crew he returned and retrieved it for us undamaged. After having had a dinghy lost overboard on the first abortive voyage to the Crozet Islands I have always carried a collapsible rubber dinghy as a spare, poor substitute though this would be for a nine-foot wooden dinghy.

That evening the gale abated, though not the rain. No one, however, flinched from the mile trudge in pouring rain which separated us from the warmth, noise, bright lights, and beer of the *Kristinemut*, the only 'local' in Godthaab and for that matter probably in all Greenland. But a gloom had been cast over the town by a disaster to a German trawler, in which twenty-six of the crew were lost, when she struck a rock outside the nearby fishing port of Faeringerhavnen when making for it in the gale that had just subsided.

Since our first visit in 1961 to Godthaab, the capital of West Greenland, the town has grown; and it is still growing. A quay for fishing boats with a fish-processing factory on it have been built at the harbour, more houses and blocks of flats have sprung up, and the long road from the harbour to the town has been surfaced. There are no seals as far south as this so that inshore fishing, the only means of livelihood for the Greenlanders, is being encouraged by building houses for the fishermen and by providing small fishing boats on easy terms. Except in the far north the Greenlanders are now a much mixed race, the original Eskimo blood mingled with that of the whalers and seamen of all the various European nations who have been in contact with Greenland over the last two or three hundred years. It would be interesting to know what the less sophisticated Eskimos whom we were to meet later at Pond Inlet, who live in tents in summer and sod and stone huts in winter, would make of life in a three-storeyed flat at Godthaab.

CHAPTER III

TO UPERNIVIK

GODTHAAB, WHICH MEANS GOOD HOPE, is an odd town. On first seeing the place, built on a barren promontory of bog and rock, surrounded by water and bleak hills, with no communications other than by sea, one wonders why it was built there. One wonders, too, how John Davis happened to make it his Greenland landfall, or why Hans Egede, the first missionary, chose it as his base. The harbour is good but small, and so hidden that anyone who did not know of it would hardly find it. Anyhow Godthaab is the capital of West Greenland and its rapid growth, with neither industry nor a surrounding population to support it, can only be accounted for by Parkinson's Law which seems to apply universally from China to Peru.

The shops of the one shopping street are well stocked and if one knows where to go all necessities and a good many luxuries can be bought at prices comparable with those of Europe. Most of the houses and flats are pre-fabricated and gaily painted. There is one large hall where a film is shown once a week and where occasional dances are held, sometimes followed by a mild brawl. One or two coffee bars, the *Kristinemut* licensed restaurant, and a small transit hotel represent the night-life. There are a church, schools, two large hospitals, and no doubt a gaol. The only surviving stone building, which is carefully preserved, is reputedly the original home of Hans Egede, the Lutheran missionary who settled there in 1721. Most of the growth is recent, for it still has the appearance of a thriving pioneer town—open drains and a forest of poles supporting a web of telephone and power lines, while bulldozers, pneumatic drills, and constant blasting, stridently announce progress.

Before leaving we stocked up with rye bread, the same colour, texture and specific gravity as black basalt, though softer, impervious to mould, nourishing, satisfying, and slightly laxative. After filling up with oil and water we sailed on June 28th with a fair wind down the fjord. We had about 500 miles to go to Upernivik which would be our last Greenland port before we headed north-west across Baffin Bay for Bylot Island another 300 miles away. Allowing a fortnight for this we still had time in hand and I had been debating the wisdom of turning aside for a week's climbing either in Godthaab Fjord or further up the coast. Bruce Reid, I noticed, had been eagerly eyeing these Godthaab mountains. On an expedition it is generally a mistake to attempt too much, to try to snatch a bonus as well as the main prize. And for all we knew, unable so far to obtain any ice information, Bylot Island might be accessible earlier than we expected. The sooner we went there to see the better.

Weather in Davis Strait is variable. In summer gales are infrequent though in this respect we had just had a sample of what it could do. Winds mostly alternate between south-east and north-west with rather too many calms in between. For most of the 30th we lay becalmed off Evigheds Fjord, the grandly mountainous fjord where we had spent a happy fortnight the previous summer. The sight of those shapely summits beckoning from afar slightly unsettled my resolve to press on. The next day a head wind of from twenty-five to thirty knots obliged us to heave to for twelve hours. How cold it was, too, while this wind whistled down from the north. By July 2nd we were on the Hellefiske Bank, the most northerly of the fishing grounds on this coast, with several trawlers and a number of the stately Portuguese schooners in sight. The Portuguese cod-fishing fleet is said to be the largest in the world comprising 72 vessels, of which 41 are the dory-carrying schooners, fishing with hand-lines, and 31 trawlers. A hospital ship accompanies the fleet. The schooners sail in April for the Newfoundland Banks and later in the season proceed to the Greenland banks to complete their catch. These dory-men inherit a long seafaring tradition of skill and hardihood, and are content and proud, even in these softer times, to follow their hard calling.

That day the noon sight put us in Lat. 66° 36′, or just north of the Arctic Circle, an event we celebrated that night with Carlsberg lager, gin, minestrone, curry, tinned fruit and chocolate sauce. Bob, the cook, was doing us well. But in my diary, in which food takes second place only to the weather, I find neither kind nor unkind references to duff. I think that in this respect he may have been lacking. We must have been too docile. Crews have mutinied with less reason:

> We haven't been but two days at sea
> When the duff it don't seem to please,
> It hadn't the richness of raisins and sichness,
> So we ups and we mutinies.

Bob, by the way, though he came from Edinburgh, hotly denied being a Scot—a refreshing trait. He had a round, red face, the redness aggravated by toiling in the galley, and the loudest laugh that I have anywhere heard. In *Mischief* on this cruise there was not that much to laugh about but that did not prevent Bob from making the rafters—or, since we are at sea, the deckhead—ring frequently. Nor was his the 'loud laugh that speaks the vacant mind' for throughout the voyage he devoted himself to one book, an uncommonly dreary, psychological treatise. Perhaps we were a solemn lot. I myself seldom utter; Ed was bowed down with meteorological cares; Stephen busy writing a masterpiece that has still to appear; Bruce flexing in vain his climbing muscles (though he had soon become a reliable hand); Mike writing short stories and tearing them up; and Bob reading himself into a psychological stupor.

A run of 104 miles on July 3rd brought us into Disko Bugt, the wide entrance to the Vaigat Channel which separates Disko Island from the mainland. As usual the bight was cluttered with icebergs of all shapes and sizes, some tabular, some like square fortresses, and others fashioned into arches and picturesque pinnacles. The Vaigat is the source of most of the icebergs that, after circling Baffin Bay, drift down the Canadian coast and finally, perhaps two years later, appear on the Newfoundland Banks. They originate in the great glaciers descending to the sea from the Greenland ice cap which, from the Vaigat northwards, extends right to the coast. It is estimated that the twelve most important glaciers in the Vaigat and northwards discharge annually some 5400 bergs. But of these only a few hundred survive to reach the Grand Banks and become a menace to shipping. South of the Vaigat the ice cap lies back from the coast leaving a strip of ice-free country varying in width from one to one hundred miles. Except in the extreme south round Julianehaab, where there is some sheep farming, this strip of ice-free land, rocky, boggy, sparsely vegetated, is of no value.

The principal settlement on Disko Island is Godhavn, a small port lying at its southern end. In the past it was the place most frequently visited by whalers and exploring ships on their voyage north. While we could hardly flatter ourselves that we were explorers, we were on our way north, so I decided to call there. According to the *Pilot* there was an Arctic Research Station at Godhavn where possibly we might get some ice information. In fact the Research Station concerned itself mainly with ecology on the land and had no curiosity whatever about ice at sea. The harbour entrance is only about a cable wide but except when icebergs are grounded in the channel, as frequently they are, presents no difficulty. The anchorage is land-locked and has a depth of seven fathoms. When we arrived on July 4th we anchored ahead of a small steamer unloading coal from Kutdlisat on the east coast of Disko Island, the only working coal mine in Greenland. This rather poor quality coal is burnt in the settlements throughout Greenland. In 1961 we sailed close by Kutdlisat. One does not look for beauty near a coal mine but I must say this place seemed to be the acme of desolation—a high, yellow cliff streaked with coal-dust, at its foot at sea level the black coal seam, a couple of dingy ships at anchor with large icebergs almost alongside, the whole shrouded in dismal fog.

We arrived on a warm, cloudless day, a day that almost persuaded the crew to believe me when I told them that the further north one went the better the weather, and how that in 1961 we had enjoyed a month of unbroken, glorious weather. We were presently boarded by the Danish manager of the shrimp-processing factory. We had been puzzled by a large vessel moored in a corner of the harbour that looked like a nineteenth-century relic, and we now learnt that this was where the shrimps were treated. She resembled the ships used by Arctic explorers in the latter half of last century, a sailing ship with an engine, clipper bows, two fully rigged masts, and between them a high funnel. She had in fact spent her life plying between Denmark and Greenland and was now ending her days moored in Godhavn boiling shrimps. This shrimping business was another attempt to find the Greenlanders profitable employment. The men caught the shrimps and sold them to the factory, while some forty girls and women were employed cleaning and packing the shrimps. I noticed that the paper bags in which the frozen shrimps were packed were marked 'Export to U.K.' Between the spacious decks all seemed to be eminently hygienic but the smell of cooked shrimps in bulk we found a bit overpowering.

Godhavn is a provincial capital and about 500 people live there. There are the usual brightly painted wooden houses, a church built in the Arctic-Byzantine style, and still a few of the old-fashioned Eskimo houses of stones with a roof of turf carrying a rich crop of grass. In the course of an evening stroll along the beach in search of the Arctic Research Station we watched Greenlanders netting fish for dog food. A few stray huskies were saving master trouble by catching their own fish but of course in this case there was no stock-piling. In winter when the sea freezes dog sledges are much in use for journeys to neighbouring settlements. Methods of dog management vary. At Holsteinborg (further south) the huskies in summer are left to feed themselves which they do in a fashion by licking the outsides of oil barrels or swimming in the harbour in search of offal from the fish factory. Seeing these voracious animals roaming the town we were surprised they did not devour some of the too numerous children who were also allowed to roam at large. At Umanak, at the north end of the Vaigat, the huskies were better off, for they were kept confined and fed once or twice a week on shark meat.

Before returning to the ship that night we found ourselves involved with the Godhavn fire brigade which presently arrived at the beach in a lorry towing a red trailer with hoses and pump to carry out a practice drill. They were led by our shrimping friend in full uniform, helmet, boots, and fireman's axe at belt. Their first target, a pit full of old sump oil, provided more trouble to set alight than to extinguish. Meantime the whole of Godhavn had arrived on the scene and were warming themselves round the second target, a huge pile of waste wood, chaffing their fire-fighting friends, trampling on the hoses, and occasionally getting hosed down as they deserved.

In spite of the absence of tourists there is in Greenland a market for curios and those who sell them are no less astute than any in Port Said, Singapore, or Katmandu. We were on the lookout for soapstone carvings and were soon boarded by a Greenlander offering some carved whalebone figures. His prices were inflexible and no doubt inflated,

Upernivik Harbour and *Mischief*

but Stephen and I were weak-minded enough to buy some of these 'tupilaks', as they are called. These grotesque, intricately carved figures are quite small representations of mythical beasts with one foot like a man's, the other a bear's paw, a bird's wing for an arm, and the head, perhaps, that of a musk ox.

To my surprise and chagrin the halcyon weather which I firmly believed had come to stay ended next day in a storm of wind and rain. The wind brought a number of small bergs into the harbour entrance where they grounded. That evening the seaplane with mail and passengers from Umanak, after circling several times, gave up and went back. The harbour is small and a seaplane has to touch down well out in the entrance which was now impeded by bergs. We had intended to sail but postponed it on account of the weather. Two young Danes from the wireless station paid us a visit and gave us the welcome news that a ship had reported meeting no ice on the way to Upernivik.

We left next day, July 7th, threading our way among the grounded bergs. Though the sea was lumpy after the previous day's blow we had a fair wind and could lay the desired course NNW. In the night the wind went round to SSE. and gave us a good run of ninety miles. With the wind dead aft we soon suffered the accidental gybe which may confidently be expected in those conditions unless the helmsman is reasonably good and extremely alert. The ship, of course, may assist by giving an untimely roll and once the helmsman allows the wind to get on the wrong side of the mainsail over goes the boom with a crash, sometimes breaking something on the way. This is commonly known as a Chinese gybe, though it is safe to assume that Chinese seamen are not more prone than others to gybing in this lubberly fashion. *Mischief* has a massive boom, massive enough to laugh at such trifling affairs as the wire guy or preventer which is rigged to prevent such accidents. Having broken the guy it swept on unimpeded to break the weather backstay as well. No further damage resulted, for the rigging is strong, as indeed it needs to be to withstand the shocks sometimes imposed on it. After this jarring experience I was content to steer two points off course thus bringing the wind well out on the quarter. It goes against the grain to steer wide when one can lay the required course. Yet on the whole nothing is lost, for the ship sails faster with the wind on the quarter and it is much safer.

The south wind brought thick weather which cleared only when the wind dropped. As it cleared we beheld a great fleet of icebergs scattered over the northern exit from the Vaigat and beyond them Ubekjendt Island and the mountains where we had spent a month in 1961. I had happy recollections of the small settlement on Ubekjendt to which we had come direct from Godthaab, and the delight we had felt to find Greenlanders wearing sealskin trousers and boots, and paddling kayaks, instead of wearing winkle-pickers and dancing the Twist. Sailing, drifting, and occasional motoring marked our slow progress. In Davis Strait light airs and fogs are a little too prevalent. They sometimes go together but neither lasts very long. There are many worse places for fog—the Straits of Belle-Isle, for instance, reputedly 'the place where they invented fog'. The calms oblige one to motor more than one likes, since the only pleasure to be had from running an engine in a small boat is the exquisite relief when it stops.

North of Ubekjendt the character of the coast changes. It is fronted by innumerable islands, behind which the ice cap approaches to the sea, and there are no mountains worthy of the name. On July 11th, a fine, clear morning, when we began to close the land, we soon descried in the distance a prominent cliff, jet black in the morning light and crowned with snow. We recognised it at once for Sanderson's Hope and the sight of this historic Arctic seamark gave me at least a tremendous thrill.

In 1587 John Davis made his third and last voyage to Davis Strait and waters beyond in search of the North-West Passage, his first having been in 1585. In all three his principal backer had been William Sanderson, a rich London merchant and a patron of exploration. Davis had three ships: *Sunneshine* which had been on the two earlier voyages, and *Elizabeth*, both of about fifty tons, and *Ellen*, a little clinker-built pinnace of only twenty tons. He felt that this third voyage should at least pay its expenses so his plan was for the three ships to sail in company to Greenland whence *Sunneshine* and *Ellen* should proceed to the Newfoundland Banks to fish while he himself would sail northwards in *Elizabeth*. At Gilbert Sound (Godthaab) *Ellen* was found to be leaking badly. Whereupon Davis took the heroically unselfish decision to dispatch the two sound vessels to the fishing grounds while he went north

Sanderson's Hope

Collecting seal from ice-floe

in the barely seaworthy *Ellen*. On June 30th the little *Ellen* lay under the shadow of this 1000-foot high cliff which Davis called 'Sanderson his Hope of a North-West Passage,' recording at the same time, 'No ice towards the north but a great sea, free, large, very salt and blue, and of an unsearchable depth.' The high hopes implied by these words were not to be realised and Sanderson's Hope proved to be their furthest north. The onset of a northerly gale prevented progress in that direction and on sailing west they soon came upon the ice of the 'middle pack' which forced them to turn south.

It is interesting to note how ice conditions change over the years or the centuries. As early as the end of June Davis had met favourable conditions and but for the northerly wind might have reached the head of Baffin Bay and anticipated the discoveries made by Baffin and Bylot in 1616. On the other hand McClintock in 1857 on his voyage in search of Franklin in the screw-yacht *Fox* (177 tons), strengthened and sheathed for ice, became iced-in on August 12th when only some eighty miles north of Upernivik, and remained in the grip of the ice until April of the next year when they were released near Holsteinborg. It is thought that ice conditions in these regions at present are generally easier than they were fifty years ago.

I noted regretfully that even on our Admiralty charts, let alone the Danish charts, the name for this historic cape is now given as 'Kaersoarssuak' and under it in brackets, in apologetically small type, is 'Sanderson's Hope'. I expect in the next edition of charts published the English name will have disappeared and we shall have only the unpronounceable Kaersoarssuak which means nothing to anyone except Greenlanders who neither need charts nor use them. Like all primitive people who are also travellers the Eskimo have names for all the features along the coast whether large or small. It is right to use these in the absence of a name with superior claims, claims that the name 'Sanderson's Hope' undoubtedly has, a name that has been used by the seamen of many European nations for 400 years, a name given to a cape that is still of importance to navigators, and a name that evokes memories of heroic men and heroic voyages. The changing of geographical names for national or political reasons goes on apace nowadays and it is of small consequence in most instances. It matters little to outsiders how often the Russians, for example, change the names of their streets, towns, or even mountains. No foreigners are allowed to climb these anyway, even if any such could overcome their repugnance sufficiently to wish to climb mountains with names like Peak Stalin or Peak of the Academy of Sciences. Upernivik is on a small island five miles north of Sanderson's Hope. There are several other islands in the vicinity and before finding our way through them we stood in under the cliff to have a good look at it. A couple of Greenlanders in a small motor boat were busy banging away at the birds that haunt the cliff, so busy that they took no notice of us. The *Arctic Pilot* (1947 edition) remarks that 'the cliff is a famous place for looms (guillemots); the birds congregate in myriads along the face...' No doubt in recent years, with the acquisition of more firearms, the Greenlanders have taken serious toll of them. The myriads have certainly been thinned, we saw only a few birds.

Sir Leopold McClintock, whose name has already been mentioned, who was one of the most successful explorers, took a lively interest in the feeding of his men, as indeed the Arctic explorer of those days had to do if he and his men were to survive. He fully realised the importance of fresh food. 'Our shooting parties', he writes, 'have twice visited a loomery and each time have brought on board 300 looms. We consider our loom soup incomparable; more like hare soup than any other, but richer, darker, and better adapted to our climate, our appetite, and consequently our tastes. So long as we had the necessary ingredients the following receipt [sic] of our excellent steward, James Gore, was strictly followed; it suited well for divers ducks, and all seabirds, especially those with dark flesh.'

Just in case any of my readers should find themselves in reduced circumstances in the neighbourhood of a loomery I append James Gore's instructions for making loom soup:

> Take 8 looms, skin and take off the two white lumps near the tail; clean and split into pieces; wash them well, also the livers. Put them into a large saucepan, cover well with water, and boil for 4 or 5 hours. An hour before serving add ½ lb of bacon cut up small, season with pepper and salt, two tablespoons of Harvey Sauce, a little Cayenne pepper, half a wineglass of lemon juice, a teaspoonful of ground

allspice, and a few cloves; thicken with 4 tablespoons of flour mixed in cold water stirred gradually into the soup. Add ½ pint of wine, after which let it boil for a few minutes. The result will be 4 quarts of rich soup.

So much for gastronome Gore. The Eskimos eat their looms raw.

CHAPTER IV

BAFFIN BAY

W E WERE BECOMING ACCUSTOMED to small harbours. At Upernivik the harbour besides being small was encumbered with rocks
and ice floes. While I was taking stock of the limited choice left by
these hazards Ed Mikeska, ready on the foredeck with the anchor, suddenly let it go. I thought we must have run aground. Apparently he
had acted on a signal, or an imagined signal, from a man on the quay,
and when one's anchor is dropped for one at the instigation of a disin-
terested spectator some confusion is bound to result. Happily at Upernivik there is no Yacht Club overlooking the harbour, with the usual
quota of eagle-eyed members, with nothing to do between drinks but
wait for some such distressing incident.

After the shouting had died down, and upon trying to move to a
proper berth, we found we had a foul anchor. With toil and sweat we
freed it by hanging it off, anchored again, and put a line ashore. There
was a small quay with a warehouse and from it four Danes presently
put off and came on board. They included the local manager for the
Royal Greenland Trading Company who by virtue of that office was
the Upernivik Pooh Bah, harbour-master, customs, health, immigra-
tion, mayor, and governor of the Province. We got out the gin but this
did not stop the manager, a stern-path-of-duty man, from asking to
see our health certificates. A regulation provides that visitors to Greenland, presumably coming by air, must have a health certificate issued
within forty-eight hours of departure. Some of us did have odd bits of
paper showing that at some distant period we had been vaccinated,
but that was all. With the assistance of more gin and some talk on our
part about the refreshing absence of red tape at Godthaab and Godhavn, and the difficulty of contracting typhoid, consumption, or small-
pox at sea, this far-flung piece of bumbledom was strangled at birth.

One of the Danes took us ashore to have coffee in his house. Compared with *Mischief's* cabin it was like an oven. Our cabin, or at any

rate the forward part of it, is heated by a small drip-feed stove using the same fuel as the engine. We asked about seals and were told that as many as 14,000 skins might be handled in a season. Upernivik in Lat. 72° 47′ is the most northern principal settlement, the centre to which sealskins are brought for disposal and from where trade goods, food, clothing, ammunition, oil etc. are distributed to small outlying settlements up or down the coast. In summer a small coasting vessel calls weekly but from November to May or June there is no communication at all.

During our very short stay we met with a lot of hospitality, having received none at all elsewhere. It is true, and I suppose only natural, that the stranger can expect a welcome only in places that are really remote. We made another friend in Peter Nissen, a Dane married to an Englishwoman, with a family of four small children at whose house we had drinks, with white bread, cheese, and Godhavn shrimps. He was keen on shooting and possessed a whole battery of firearms. When he heard that we had no weapons on board he was distressed and insisted, much against my will, in lending a .306 American service rifle. It was dated 1917 and looked as if it had never been fired. He talked of our shooting seals with it, or even polar bears, thinking perhaps that we might need some protection when crossing Bylot Island. He worked in the radio station and thanks to him we obtained an ice report from Baffin Bay through the Danish liaison officer at Thule, the American base some 300 miles to the north.

Having arrived on July 11th we sailed on the afternoon of the 13th. A few houses, the hospital, and the Greenland Company's trading store just about exhausted the sights. We spent some hours patiently fishing with a grapnel for the gash bucket which Stephen had thrown overboard. We watched with interest, too, the methods used to supply the place with drinking water. A launch went out—it had not far to go—and having grappled an ice floe or bergy bit of several tons towed it to the beach. There a lorry awaited with a gang of men who attacked the ice with picks and crowbars to break it into small pieces which were then put in sacks for the lorry to distribute to the various houses. We ourselves, in need of some thirty gallons of water, were kindly allowed to draw on the hospital where they had facilities for melting ice in quantity. The island is waterless; considering, too, the poor harbour, one wonders how it came to be chosen as a settlement. I suppose even if there were a lake or a stream the water would not remain unfrozen for many months in the year. For seventy-nine days in the year the sun does not so much as rise. When we were there the air temperature was 65° and the sea 39°.

The ice report which we had received from Thule in slightly garbled form seemed to indicate Lat. 74° as the northern limit of ice. In Davis Strait and Baffin Bay there are two main ice bodies. There is what is known as the 'East Ice' which in winter and spring drifts round Cape Farewell and up the coast, generally disappearing before it reaches as far as Godthaab. And there is the 'West Ice', the ice carried southwards by the Arctic or Labrador current consisting of ancient floes of great thickness which come from the Polar Sea through Smith, Jones, and Lancaster sounds, mixed up with icebergs and the ice which forms each winter in Baffin Bay and Davis Strait. In winter this ice extends and meets with the ice forming along the Greenland coast north of Disko so that the whole sea is covered.

In April the ice on the Greenland side begins to open and besides this there is nearly always a large area of more or less open water in the northern part of Baffin Bay. This 'polynia', as it is called, is known as the 'North Water' and for two centuries whalers and explorers have been aware of its existence and have taken advantage of it. Its origin is still not definitely known. By July, in an average year, the North Water is no longer isolated and can easily be reached by the widening belt of open water along the Greenland coast. In April and May the ice from Upernivik northwards might well be impenetrable so that the North Water could not be reached. The whalers of the previous century used to make it their aim to reach the North Water as early in the season as possible—in May or at latest June—by forcing their way through the ice north of Upernivik. In these attempts it was by no means unusual for ships to be beset, nipped, and sunk; they always sailed in company so that if a ship sank the crew who had taken refuge on the ice would be picked up by another. But even in mid-summer there generally remains a huge, pear-shaped extent of ice floes reaching from the southern edge of the North Water down to the narrowest part of Davis Strait in about Lat. 64°. This is known as the 'Middle Pack'.

In order to avoid the Middle Pack we should have to reach the North Water before shaping a course for Bylot Island. For a whaling ship mid-July would have been fully late but by small-boat standards it might be too early in the season. And supposing Baffin Bay to be successfully crossed, would the ice in Lancaster Sound and Pond Inlet allow us to reach the coast of Bylot Island? The distance was about 360 miles. If we had to dodge about a lot to avoid ice, steering the sort of course that would make an eel dizzy, it might well be half as much again. Steering a course depends upon the compass and I had already noted that the Canadian chart of those waters bore the discouraging warning that 'The magnetic compass is useless in this region.'

At Upernivik the magnetic variation is already 60°W., at Bylot Island it increases to 75°W., and at the western end of Lancaster Sound it is 90°W. The magnetic pole is at present roughly in Lat. 70°N. Long. 97°W., only some 400 miles from Bylot Island in a south-westerly direction. At the magnetic pole a freely suspended compass needle points up and down having no horizontal force to give it direction. Hence the extreme sluggishness of the compass needle in the Canadian Arctic and its complete uselessness near the magnetic pole. And as a matter of interest, should anyone who reads this be contemplating a journey from the magnetic pole to the true north pole, they will find they will have to steer due south by compass to reach it.

We had, of course, already noticed the increasing unwillingness of our little five-inch compass card to move, but having moved it did point in the right direction. Had it not brought us more or less unerringly to Upernivik? Going west to Bylot Island the horizontal force would become less and less and the compass correspondingly less inclined to bestir itself. However, long before the day of the gyro compass and radar aids, many ships with compasses no better than ours had navigated these waters and we hoped we could manage as well.

We sailed slowly away from Upernivik on a lovely, calm, sunny evening, the placid sea dotted with immaculate icebergs, rocky islets glowing warmly in the setting sun, and astern of us the distant line of the ice cap faintly tinged with yellow.

Even on the more southerly part of the Greenland coast one can only identify one's position vaguely by mountains or the openings to fjords. North of Upernivik there are not even these to provide a clue.

Between Sanderson's Hope and an 1800-foot-high pillar known as the Devil's Thumb 100 miles to the north, the coast presents the same front of indistinguishable islands and featureless ice cap. We steered northwest aiming to reach Lat. 74° where, if the Thule ice report was right, we might be able to turn west. At midnight when ice appeared ahead we turned north and soon lost sight of what must have been a detached raft of floes and not the edge of the Middle Pack. By noon of the 14th we were in Lat. 73° 23′ N. 58° W. with no ice anywhere in sight.

That we managed to get ourselves into trouble the very next day was my own fault. Having met some loose floes, less than 4/10 ice cover, I assumed that this was merely another detached raft and began to weave a way through it in a general northwesterly direction. The amount of open water soon began to diminish. We headed northwards and that was no good. Finally we were forced to retreat eastwards and it was late evening before we were clear of the ice, back in square one, having wasted the best part of a day. The night was very cold, the air temperature 32° and the sea 33°. By morning, when we had got well away from the ice, the sea temperature had risen to 35°. Though the presence of an iceberg does not affect the sea or air temperature, the near presence of large quantities of pack-ice has a marked effect. On a day of little wind and a lot of fog the halyards became festooned with icicles and frozen rime. The ice had to be shaken off before the halyards would render through the blocks.

The 17th was yet another day of fog and calms, not a ripple on the water, and so still that the creaking of a bird's wings as it flew by invisibly in the fog could easily be heard. In spite of the comparative warmth, sea and air temperature both at 36°, our halyards were thick with ice while the baggywrinkle (the anti-chafe gear wrapped round shrouds and topping lifts) looked like elongated snowballs. Having motored for six hours we felt we had done enough. The fog certainly increased the tension. For all we could tell we might have been motoring steadily into an ice cul-de-sac. But on the whole we were content. The cabin felt all the warmer when one came off watch and we did not mind having ice on the rigging provided the sea remained free.

On the 18th, when by dead reckoning we had reached Lat. 74° 40′, we met with ice all along our port hand. For two hours we steered north along the edge until I grew impatient and decided to try conclusions with what after all might be merely a narrow line of floes—much to the dismay of Ed who had a wholesome respect for ice having spent some time bashing through it in an ice-breaker. Forewarned by recent experience I did not persevere too long. We turned north-east and soon reached open water again. On a day of little wind, the sea calm, in a region of no strong currents, there is no danger in poking about among loose floes always provided one has room to turn. *Mischief* unfortunately needs a lot of space in which to turn. But it would be unwise to persevere long amongst ice floes without being able to see open water ahead or at any rate quite certain it was there. On a day of wind, the sea rough, and the ice on the move, it would be courting disaster to be amongst it in a small, unprotected vessel. That day we saw a number of seals on the floes and I was glad they had the sense to dive into the water before we got close enough for a shot.

In the night we had some wind and made good eight miles to the west. All morning the light wind held, increasing to a fresh breeze by afternoon. The sun peering vaguely through the overcast enabled me to take a sight which put us in 75° N. 66° W., about halfway across Baffin Bay. Ice then appeared about a mile away on the port hand but so far our progress had been fairly painless. It looked now as if we had reached the North Water and that the ice showing up to the south must be the edge of the Middle Pack. When ice appeared dead ahead late in the evening our hope momentarily died but having come up with it we found it to be merely a long line of scattered floes projecting from the main body of the pack. Beyond lay more open water. In climbing it is notoriously a mistake to write off by mere inspection a seemingly impossible route. One must come to grips with it. In the same way ice floes that in fact are widely scattered, when seen from even half a mile away from the deck of a small boat—or even from the crosstrees— appear just as unbroken and impenetrable as heavily congested pack-ice. All next day in light winds and showers of sleet we sailed west over perfectly open water, only a strong iceblink to the south denoting the whereabouts of the pack. The sun made a fitful appearance and our noon position I put at 74° 40′ N. 66° 40′ W. There happened that day to be a partial eclipse, so that we were delighted when the sky cleared to allow us to watch the progress of the shadow which began at 5 p.m. and lasted until 7 p.m. A huge iceberg afforded us another remarkable spectacle by heaving itself majestically out of the water as if about to capsize. At each ponderous roll one side lifted and the other sank by twenty to thirty feet. By estimating the number of cricket pitches that could be placed on it end to end some of us reckoned it about 300 feet long, others 500 feet. This led to arguments about its tonnage and estimates varied even more widely from a million tons to ten million. There is scope enough for error because the proportion of ice above water to that below varies greatly with the type of berg. A blocky, precipitous-sided berg has about five times more of its volume below water, than above, while a much pinnacled, so-called 'picturesque' berg, has only twice as much. As I write this, surrounded by slide rules and assisted by a young relative familiar with hypothetical logarithms and hyperbolic functions, I have worked the sum afresh and find that our rolling iceberg, give or take a few tons, weighed 450,000 tons.

In the evening iceblink could be seen ahead as well as to the south. Ed swore there was ice to the north, too—ice all round, in fact. But he took the same lugubrious view of ice as he did of the weather. Having read more than once *Letters from High Latitudes* and being familiar with it, I was reminded of Wilson, Lord Dufferin's personal servant, who moved uneasily about the deck with the air of Cassandra at the conflagration of Troy. Cassandra Wilson used to wake his master something in this fashion:

> 'Seven o'clock, my Lord.'
> 'Very well. How's the wind?'
> 'Blowing a gale, my Lord—dead ahead.'
> 'How many points is she off her course?'
> 'Four points, my Lord—full four points.'
> 'Is it pretty clear, Wilson?'
> 'Can't see your hand, my Lord—can't see your hand.'
> 'Much ice in sight?'
> 'Ice all round, my Lord—ice all round.'

At midnight we came up with the ice that earlier had been betrayed to us by the 'blink', a yellowish-white appearance of the sky produced by the reflection of pack-ice on the clouds. It proved to be another projecting cape which we presently rounded and resumed our westerly course. Throughout that next day we met scattered floes, so widely scattered that for the most part we could maintain our course. From sights I reckoned we had about 120 miles to go. Seals were fairly plentiful, sticking their heads out of the water or basking peacefully on the floes, and since we were under sail the latter took little notice of our passing. The crew seemed anxious to have one shot and equally in favour of casting me in the role of murderer. I must have been talking too much of my misspent youth in East Africa, of elephants and rhino, for they evidently took me for Buffalo Bill, or such a marksman as the famous elephant hunter Neumann who, because he invariably killed all his game with the one shot, earned from his Swahili followers the sobriquet *Risasi moja*—one cartridge.

When voyaging single-handed through the Patagonian channels Slocum felt that in the loneliness of those waters life of any kind should be held sacrosanct. I, too, felt reluctant to reduce the seal population by even one. But public opinion was too strong so, consoling myself with thoughts of fresh meat, I took Nissen's rifle, from which no shot had yet been fired, and lay down in the bows. It would not do to bungle it, the eyes of England, so to speak, were upon me. Waiting until the ship had glided quietly to within about a hundred yards of our unsuspecting victim, I fired. The seal hardly moved. It had either been killed outright or very hard hit, but I gave it one more round to make sure it did not slip away into the sea.

We hove to, launched the dinghy, and Bruce and Mike went off with rope and ice-axe to retrieve the body. The ice-axe was needed to cut a landing place on the floe. It proved to be a big harp seal. Stephen made a good job of skinning it and then put together a wooden frame where he stretched the skin to dry. The skinning is comparatively easy but cleaning a sealskin, removing all traces of blubber, is most laborious and troublesome for the amateur. With various implements we whittled away day by day and still there were bits of blubber all over the skin. Finally it was left for the expert hands of an Eskimo at Pond Inlet who quickly made a proper job of it.

We enjoyed the liver and we dutifully ate what little edible meat there was. To enjoy seal meat, perhaps one should be sitting in an igloo or smoke-blackened hut after a day's sledging, a blizzard raging outside, devouring it in one's fingers after slightly warming and smoking it over a blubber lamp.

On July 22nd we ran all day through patches of fog before a light wind. Both fog and wind increased at night (there was, of course, no darkness) till we were reaching at five knots with a spanking breeze at north. Seeing a few floes about we put an extra man on watch. At 1 a.m. the fog cleared and at 2 a.m. (ship's time) I took a meridian sight of the sun in the north. True the sun was too low for a reliable sight but I liked the notion of taking a meridian sight in the middle of the night. On a fine, clear morning a bank of cloud away to the west hinted at the presence of land.

Before the weather closed down again, as it did before noon of the 23rd, I thought we had about forty miles to go to Cape Liverpool at the north-east corner of Bylot Island. At 4 p.m. I got a snap sight which was probably useless on account of the fog, but taking everything into account I reckoned we were only about twelve miles from the cape. Whereupon I altered course to WSW. hoping to fetch the land near Maud Bight which is twenty miles west of the cape and well inside Lancaster Sound. In view of the probability of ice in the sound, the reputed uselessness of the compass, and the paucity of reliable sights, this was a considerable act of faith. We were certainly near some part of the Canadian Arctic, we might even fetch the coast of Bylot Island. Beyond that it was anybody's guess.

> Beyond the clouds, beyond the waves that roar,
> There may indeed, or may not be, a shore.

About an hour later, the fog still thick and Ed on deck steering, the rest of us below were startled by an agonised yell, a yell like that from a covey of angry screech owls giving tongue together. Whether it heralded triumph or disaster I could not determine but knowing who had uttered it I surmised the latter. Tumbling up on deck we saw, a short 200 yards away, at about the limit of visibility, a low range of sandhills.

CHAPTER V

BYLOT ISLAND

———◆———

I N LECKY'S *WRINKLES*, of which I had a copy on board, there is a
remark to the effect that 'there is nothing so distressing as running
on shore, unless there is also present some doubt as to which continent
the shore belongs.' We were not quite in that predicament. We were
comfortably far from the beach—we had lost no time in anchoring—
and in my opinion this was undoubtedly Bylot Island, though what
part of it was, of course, a question.

Taking a map of the island I rowed the dinghy ashore. Not that I
expected to meet any natives, hostile or friendly, of whom I might ask
our whereabouts, or even any of the notices found nowadays on most
beaches—'Deck Chairs 2d.', or 'Bathing Prohibited'. But on the map
which, with regard to the coastline, is pretty detailed, there might be
some identifiable features. Just west of Cape Liverpool, for instance,
there was marked a lagoon where a river debouched. The cape itself is
not significant enough, it is merely a bend in the coastline, a slight pro-
tuberance, as Dr Johnson might have called it. As far as could be seen
in the fog the coast ran straight roughly from south-east to north-west,
as the coast near Cape Liverpool does run. In a hurried walk along the
beach in both directions I met several small streams and finally a back-
water which a liberal-minded man might have called a lagoon. Back on
board, with more confidence than I really felt, I assured the crew we
were off Cape Liverpool. After supper some of us landed again for further exploration. The fog remained thick and apart from some old bear
tracks we saw nothing else of interest. We set an anchor watch.

Though we could make Cape Liverpool our starting point for
crossing the island, Bruce and I preferred if possible to start from
Maud Bight, twenty miles further west, where a large glacier came
right down to the coast, thus offering a broad highway to the interior.
At this time of year at that low level the glacier, we thought, would
almost certainly have a surface of dry ice, free from snow, on which we

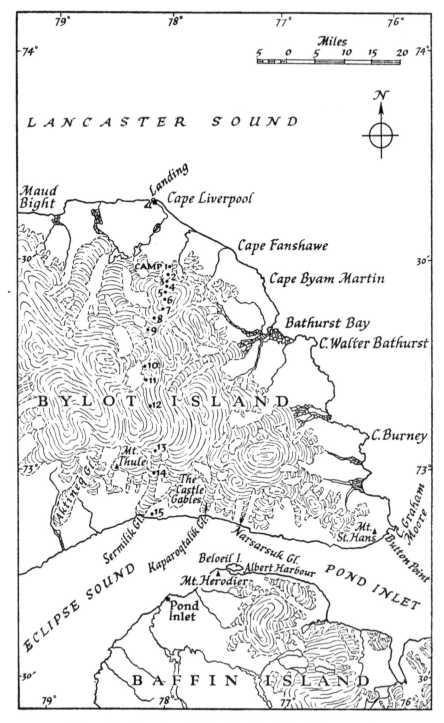

Map 2: The Crossing of Bylot Island, 25 July–8 August 1963

would be able to move at a good pace. At Cape Liverpool the nearest glacier was eight miles away from the beach.

Early on the 24th—the fog as thick as ever—we got our anchor and started sailing a little north of west with a good breeze at north. Very soon we began meeting icebergs and large flat floes, evidently at the entrance to Lancaster Sound. With one of these we had a terribly close shave. In the absence of any visible land it was difficult to tell whether we were being set up or down by any current. Stephen was at the helm pointing reasonably clear of a 100-foot-high ice monster with a ram like a battleship. Only when we drew near did I realise that we were being set down towards it very fast indeed. By then we were too close either to gybe or to go about. We could only hold on and pray that we were going fast enough to miss it. We shot by with about ten feet to spare. My knees still knock when I think of this near miss.

When the sun showed at 10 a.m., the horizon below it seemingly clear enough for a sight, I took one which showed that we were about ten miles east of our assumed position. My ideas about Cape Liverpool had to be revised. We must have been well to the south-east of it. The clearing, during which we had seen no land, lasted but a short time. Tacking towards the land we met more floes, stood out again, and continued tacking off and on until the wind died. Having started the engine we once more closed the land where we could make out fast ice (winter ice still fast to the shore) and beyond, very dimly, a low coast-line. As we followed the edge of the fast ice westwards we were gradually forced away from the shore by its increasing width until finally the fast shore ice merged with heavy floes and blocked the sound. At 6 p.m. we had to abandon any hope of reaching Maud Bight or of penetrating any further west in Lancaster Sound.

Coasting back along the edge of the fast ice, keeping a sharp lookout for seals, polar bears, and somewhere to anchor, at last at 8.30 p.m. we found a little ice-free hole where a river debouched. We anchored there, only a few yards from the shore, with fast ice on either side of us. The strong current from the river which had kept the opening clear of ice also prevented us from swinging. We had barely done congratulating ourselves on finding this snug hole when the fog rolled away in dramatic fashion, revealing a wide stretch of brown tundra and beyond it a tangle of snow mountains brilliantly lit by the westering sun. A

Anchorage in Lancaster Sound, off Cape Liverpool

hasty inspection of our surroundings showed that the river formed an undoubted lagoon and that its course, parallel to the coast, agreed with that on the map near Cape Liverpool. This was decisive. We had already had more luck than we deserved and I had no mind to push it any further by trying to force our way to Maud Bight. As Swift said: 'There is no piece of knowledge in fewer hands than that of knowing when to have done.' Bruce and I could very well start our journey from here and we had already marked down a glacier that would take us inland. Naturally the crew were all agog to set foot at once upon this barren and almost unknown shore. They proposed a walk after supper and for once I was quick enough to seize the advantage. Their energy could be harnessed. 'When they bring you a heifer be ready with the rope', as Sancho Panza was fond of saying. Accordingly Bruce and I quickly made up some light loads which we carried inland for a mile and a half where we dumped them. On returning to the ship I took a sight, hoping to verify our position. Either I was too tired or there was too much refraction, for the working of it made no sense at all.

In contrast to the general run of the weather ever since Upernivik, and especially of the last few days, we enjoyed on July 25th and for several subsequent days bright, cloudless weather. There were no flowers and hardly any birds to rejoice and sing but even the bleak tundra assumed a more kindly aspect. But the thin ice that formed overnight round the ship reminded us of how far north we were and of the briefness of the arctic summer. I considered food for eighteen days a sufficiently liberal allowance for Bruce and I to take for the fifty-mile crossing. One had to assume that nothing untoward would befall either of us and that the boat would be there to pick us up. Food, together with our personal loads, tent, cooking gear, paraffin, and rope would, we reckoned, add up to about 160 lbs. The 15-lb tent was a big item and I had canvassed the idea of sleeping in snow-holes. But I like my comfort and in view of the sort of snow we were to encounter I am glad we did not try. Many years ago I may have been able to stagger downhill under an 80-lb load, and judging by what one reads in climbing journals this seems nowadays to be a standard load, especially among New Zealand climbers. One sometimes wonders whether the loads are weighed or whether they merely feel like 80 lbs—as indeed I could swear was the weight of any load that I now attempt to carry.

However, on this journey I had no intention of competing in a weight-carrying contest. About 40 lb would be more than enough and the idea of adding to it by taking Peter Nissen's rifle never so much as crossed my mind. We hoped that for the first march, with the help of two volunteers, we could carry everything as far as the glacier. After that we should have to relay until we had consumed enough to be able to carry what was left in one lift.

Accordingly on the 25th Bruce and I, Stephen and Bob, set out for the foot of the glacier about eight miles away. Ed had the job of taking *Mischief* round to the settlement in Pond Inlet and I felt she could not be in safer or more capable hands. The settlement is on the south or Baffin Island side of Pond Inlet, more or less opposite and separated by ten miles of water from the snout of the Sermilik glacier, the glacier by which Bruce and I hoped to descend to the south coast. The Sermilik is one of four glaciers on the south coast which have names. These and Mt Thule are about the only names on the map apart from the capes and bays of the coastline. I told Ed that we expected to reach the south coast about August 12th and that on either side of that date he was to look out for smoke signals at 8 a.m. and noon. If after the lapse of a week nothing had been seen he would have to sail over and look for us up the Sermilik. On shore we had noticed nothing much with which to make smoke. Perhaps on the south side there would be more vegetation, at the worst we could burn the tent.

Bunyan relates in one of his dreams: 'I saw a man clothed in rags and a great burden upon his back.' I thought of this as I watched Bob, all enthusiasm, setting off that morning. He had joined the ship with remarkably little clothing and now that little was fast becoming rags. But he did have a pair of new climbing boots, a pair which he had worn only once before for a very short time the previous evening. At the dump we added that to our loads and set off again. The going was perfectly flat and reasonably smooth, interspersed with patches of bog which had to be avoided. A mouse and a pure white snowy owl were the only signs of life.

Besides his threadbare clothes Bob seemed bent on mortifying the flesh through the stomach. When we called a halt for lunch he produced for his own consumption merely two pieces of very dry black bread. But shortly after he was in real trouble, his new boots having begun to hurt so much that he had to take them off and walk in his socks. True he had on two thick pairs but I realised that very soon he would have to be told to go back, for he was not the kind to give in willingly. We then came to the only obstacle of the day, a fairly fast-flowing river about knee-deep. Stephen and I made the mistake of crossing barefoot. The stones on the bottom were slippery and half-way over both of us took a ducking. Profiting by our example Bruce crossed in his boots. Bob had no choice, his boots being too painful to wear, and when we were all across I sent him back.

The flat tundra now came to an end. We began toiling up a boulder fan, the debris deposited by the glacier above. Our pace became slower and slower, the heat of the day and our weeks of inaction on the boat taking their toll. Stephen had still to return and obviously we were not going to reach the glacier, so at 5 p.m., having found a tent site and water, we called it a day. Stephen started back at once while Bruce and I, after pitching the tent and making a brew, went back to fetch Bob's load. The huge, erratic boulder by which it had been left looked a long way off and it was two hours before we were back, intent on our supper. On this and on every succeeding day we had a one-lb tin of pemmican between the two of us, as thick, rich, and ·satisfying a brew as can be imagined. According to a pocket aneroid the height was 800 feet.

The morning dawned fine and clear. We could see right across the ice-filled Lancaster Sound to North Devon Island, low and comparatively free from snow. *Mischief* had gone. We had, so to speak, burnt our boats. Now it was 'Pike's Peak or bust'. How mistaken can one be? We had looked forward eagerly and confidently to setting foot on the glacier where, we assumed, we should tread dry ice or crisp, firm snow. Upon reaching it we sank almost at once into soft snow eighteen inches deep with water underneath. This seemed too bad to be true. We tried the middle of the glacier and found it no better; the side, and that was worse. The digust we felt at this belying of our hopes presently turned to misgiving. How were we to carry loads for fifty miles through this sort of stuff in eighteen days? As target for the day we set our eyes on a rock spur round which the glacier bent out of sight. By 2 p.m., when still well short of it, we had had enough and made camp in the snow alongside a flat boulder almost as big as a

Bylot Island, preparing to camp on the glacier

Bylot Island, Camp X (4350 ft.)

table. It would not quite accomodate the tent which we had to pitch in slushy snow where the deeper one dug the wetter it became. Fortified by strong tea we started back for the remaining loads and were home again by 6 p.m.

The rock spur where Camp II should have been put finally served for Camp III. The going continued to be deplorable except for a short half mile of south-facing slope which the sun had stripped bare of snow where our speed in comparison became that of an express. The leader, by treading cat-like, might remain on top for a few yards, then down he would go thigh-deep with both feet in water to thresh about like a fly in a jam-pot. The man behind fared no better, for a step that had supported the leader generally collapsed when used for the second time. However, we kept moving. As the proverb says, 'be not afraid of going slowly, be only afraid of standing still.' One blessing was the entire absence of crevasses which enabled us to move unroped. We were already 2550 feet above sea level and we camped a bit early that day on account of mist and rain. There must have been something very peculiar about atmospheric conditions outside. In the course of many hours spent in small tents at all levels, from sea level to 27,000 feet, I have never before encountered such an opaque atmosphere, or fug, inside a tent. Our wet clothes were steaming, the cooking pot was steaming, and I had a pipe going—all, of course, normal conditions— yet I could hardly see Bruce's face lying alongside me, while the far end of the tent seven feet away was completely obscured. When the rain stopped we went back for the loads.

We failed to reach our objective for the fourth day, a distant snow col, by the usual large margin. At midday we took advantage of a bare boulder-strewn slope to make camp. The toil of shifting rocks to build a platform was a small price to pay for a dry lodging. We were here 3000 feet up. We kept assuring ourselves that the snow was improving, an assurance as often belied when one of us disappeared up to the waist. The constant expectation of suddenly sinking like this was almost as bad as the reality; like at the old fun fairs where for threepence one could enter a haunted house and have one's nerves stretched in a variety of ways, including a dark, narrow corridor where the floor suddenly collapsed. At this camp, while hacking out some ice to melt for water, Bruce broke the shaft of my ice-axe. Bound with a strip of tin and multiple lashings it served well enough for probing snow. There seemed not the remotest chance of our having to use an axe to cut steps.

We reached the snow col (3600 feet) the next day, July 29th, after a hard yet satisfying day. Each trip, the first, and the second to relay the loads forward, took four hours. At this height the snow proved less consistently bad; we thought seventy-five per cent of it to be relatively good and the rest infernally bad. A few minutes after starting we were always wet to the waist. So far our view had been restricted to the snow ridges either side of the glacier; there were no moraines at the side of the glacier and the snow on it merely merged with the snow of the slope leading up to the ridge. But from the col we enjoyed a long vista down a wide glacier to the sea beyond, probably the glacier descending to Maud Bight. Our route from the col started with a descent to another glacier basin. Thus emboldened we set off with double loads but we soon abandoned them after reaching the treacherous snow in the basin. Again we found a bit of rock to camp on at 1 p.m. before returning to retrieve the remaining loads. We had lost some height, this Camp VII being only 2800 feet. Although we studied the map avidly and marked on it each day where we thought we were it was of no help in finding a route. The snow-field which we were traversing appears on the map as a mass of vague form lines and none of the glaciers are identifiable except when they approach the coast. Thus we had at least the satisfaction of finding our own way through unmapped country. We steered south by the sun, selecting some feature that lay roughly in that direction and making for it by the line of least resistance. Had we kept to the ridges we might have avoided losing any height but we should not have found any of those patches of snow-free slopes which afforded such exquisite relief from the snow bog.

We made Camp VIII on August 1st after what we considered a good day. Thanks to some stretches of bare ice we had made good at least three miles. Nevertheless we were obliged to pitch the tent in the middle of a snow-field with not a rock in sight. We met a new and formidable obstacle in the shape of streams that in their meandering course through the wide snow-field had worn a six-foot furrow down to blue ice and had cast up on either side a high bank of snow. I tried walking for a time without snow glasses and suffered for it with a mild touch of snow-blindness.

For the first time we managed to carry all the gear in one lift to the next camp, still at only 2800 feet. Several deep furrows had to be crossed, usually necessitating making a cast up or down stream until we found a place narrow enough to jump. There was no future at all in setting foot on the slippery ice in the fast running water. Once Bruce did incautiously put a foot in and I had to hang on to him to prevent his being swept off his feet. Camp IX was an oasis in a snow desert, a delightful site with a ready-made gravel platform, a few tufts of grass, yellow poppies, a pair of pipits, a butterfly, and at our feet a clear blue tarn. Moreover the day was hot and cloudless, so still that at our lunch halt we brewed tea on an unshielded stove in the open air. In the evening we had tea outside in our garden, admiring what was almost a mountain prospect, the level snow stretching away to a distant serrated ridge.

Once more we began making height, camping on August 3rd at 3600 feet. Having only the one trip to make we kept moving until we had covered the record distance of five miles. But we had our troubles. Bruce now began to find his boots hurting him, so much so that he soon became quite crippled. They were Italian climbing boots with a piece of metal inserted to stiffen the heel, and short of pulling the boots to pieces to remove the metal there was nothing we could do. Then when nearing camp—I must have been tired and careless—I came a cropper on a loose boulder and savaged my left arm. Nothing was broken but for the next two days it was quite useless. Anyway the incident served as a caution.

That night it actually froze. On account of my arm Bruce had most of the packing up to do, but when at length we started we enjoyed for a short time the pleasure of walking on hard, crisp snow. What with Bruce's boots and my arm neither of us felt like a long day so we camped early at a height of 4350 feet. A col that we hoped might be the watershed appeared to be only about two miles away. At this height we were in cloud and mist and for a time saw no guiding sun.

Starting on August 5th we steered at first by a rock outcrop looming vaguely through the mist and when this became obscured we had to resort to a prismatic compass. I sent Bruce ahead on a bearing until he had disappeared in the mist where he stopped and waited for me to come up. Climbing steadily all the time we reached the col early in the afternoon at a height of 5700 feet. By then the cloud had dispersed and we estimated the height of a nearby, rounded snow summit to be about 6500 feet. This might well have been the highest or one of the highest points of Bylot Island but neither of us had the inclination or the energy to make the long snow plod to the top.

This col was undoubtedly on the watershed and it behove us to be careful about our next move. A moderately steep slope dropped 500 feet to a snow basin, the main source of a big glacier which disappeared round a shoulder of the mountain. We half suspected this glacier to be the Sermilik. If it were then we were home and dry. But it appeared to run too much east of south, so before committing ourselves and losing precious height by a descent to the basin we began traversing towards another col lying due south. Luckily for us the snow of the traverse proved so vile that we soon gave up in despair and began plunging recklessly downhill. 'No matter where it leads me, the downhill path for me' was no doubt in both our minds. Whatever this glacier might prove to be it would certainly conduct us to the coast. We camped in the basin at a height of 5200 feet.

We were 'with child', as Pepys would say, to see round the corner so that we should know in what direction the glacier trended. How-ever, making the best speed we could on the morning of August 6th we failed to reach the corner before a great cloud advanced up the glacier to blot out everything. Once more we had to use the compass. Owing to the advance of day and the gradual loss of height, the hard crust on which we had started walking began to soften. Soon we were sinking and floundering every few steps. At last, however, we had turned the corner and far away, through a brief clearing of the cloud, I felt sure I had caught a glimpse of blue, a blue that could not be mistaken for sky. With some difficulty I refrained from crying out, as I should have done, 'The sea! The sea!' I did not want to raise false hopes in Bruce who by now, thanks to his wretched boots, had his work cut out to keep going. The glacier led south so that we were pretty sure it was the Sermilik and we felt pleased at having hit it off so nicely. Lured on by some dis-tant rocks on the left bank we made tremendous efforts to reach them, wading through snow just as bad as that which we had met at the start of our journey. We dumped the loads with the idea of first breaking a trail to the rocks and then returning for the loads. It was no use, we were too tired. After a mile the rocks looked no nearer. We gave in, fetched the loads, and made camp in the snow. The height was 3700 feet.

We were nearly out of the wood. On August 7th after two more hours in really hellish snow we won through to dry ice and our troubles were over. Provided *Mischief* had reached Pond Inlet we did not think there would be any delay in our being taken off. With the sea now in view we pressed on and camped finally on a moraine, the first we had seen. We might as well have stayed on the glacier itself, for on removing some stones and gravel to make a platform we exposed the ice beneath. My air mattress had long been useless so I lay on top of a Yukon pack-board and kept pretty warm. This last camp but one was at 2200 feet and some seven or eight miles from the coast. We thought that by making an early start we might reach the sea before midday in time to send up the first prearranged smoke signal to let the crew know we had arrived.

So on August 8th at 6.30 a.m. off we went with light loads, downhill, and on dry ice. Tired though we both were and with Bruce limping along behind, surely we could make it before noon. At last the time came to quit the glacier which terminated several hundred yards from the sea, and at last the rope which we had carried without having occasion to use came in handy for us to rope down a fifteen-foot cliff of ice at the edge of the glacier. There we first set foot on dry land, so to speak, after a voyage of fourteen days over snow. The last seven miles had taken five hours. We need not have hurried. The whole Baffin Island coast lay covered in cloud.

CHAPTER VI

POND INLET

———◆———

A T ITS SNOUT THE SERMILIK glacier is over a mile wide. Only the western corner of it is still washed by the sea, for it is receding and has been receding for a long time as the huge and very old moraine on the left bank showed. It took us a long time to climb this moraine and having reached the top we saw what in our snow-weary eyes looked like a lush meadow. What a contrast, too, was here from the bare, brown, stony waste that borders the north coast. Besides grass and a few flowers we noted with satisfaction an abundant growth of heath that promised to make for us a lot of smoke. Having carefully chosen a site, before erecting the tent we layed down a springy mattress of heath. We promised ourselves soft lying after what I think, taken all in all, had been the hardest fifty miles I had ever done, certainly the slowest. If we were not now in ecstasy it was at least comfort.

We had put the tent about 300 feet above the beach, fully high enough for a fire to be seen from sea level at ten miles distance provided someone looked for it in the right direction at the right time. Tired limbs and a cold east wind kept us inside except for the time spent gathering a supply of heath for the fire. Although the next morning broke fine, a bank of fog still hid the opposite coast. When it cleared later we could make out even with unaided eyes the square outlines of buildings and a steamer at anchor. She was making a lot of smoke, evidently preparatory to sailing, for she presently moved off westwards towards Eclipse Sound. We guessed she must be the annual supply ship visiting the settlements at Pond Inlet, Arctic Bay in Admiralty Inlet, and Resolute on Cornwallis Island. We spent the morning building a big cairn on the beach and gathering driftwood to augment the fire. At noon the great moment had come. It was a substantial blaze comparable, we imagined, to the beacons signalling the arrival of the Armada and, we hoped, with an equally galvanizing effect. For what it was worth we also flashed a mirror and then settled back confidently to wait. An hour elapsed and nothing happened. Except for a few lonely icebergs the ten-mile stretch of water remained obstinately blank.

In the afternoon I took a walk uphill and then gained the beach below Castle Gables by way of a steep gully. As we had guessed from the air photographs this peak is merely a serrated ridge of rotten rock. Walking back by the beach I found evidence of old camp sites— a sheltering wall of stones, tins, bits of box-wood—relics perhaps of the American party of 1954. I collected more driftwood. At noon there had been a lot of wind blowing the smoke away horizontally, so that evening when the air was still we made more smoke.

On the next day we varied our tactics, lighting three fires in widely separated places instead of one big blaze. We had them going just in time, as a belt of fog crept slowly westwards along the Baffin Island coast. Albert Harbour, the best anchorage in Pond Inlet ten miles east of the settlement, had already been blotted out. We were already a little puzzled and as we gazed across the sunlit, smiling sea where nothing moved we debated the absence of response to our signals. If they had chosen to lie at Albert Harbour they would not have seen our smoke that day and might be too far off anyway. But it was unlikely that the crew would stop long at that empty harbour, however good the anchorage, with the hospitality of the settlement and fresh faces so close at hand. We found it hard, too, to believe that our smoke was not visible from the settlement or had not been noticed. Besides the crew who would be looking out, there would be numbers of keen-eyed Eskimos, quick to spot anything unusual, and probably with nothing better to do than ourselves but stare across the sea. There remained only the disturbing possibility that *Mischief* had not arrived, that she had been delayed for some reason, or even caught in the ice. There was no ice in sight now but a fortnight earlier conditions might have been as bad or worse than those we had encountered in Lancaster Sound.

As a result of these reflections we took stock of our food. The few luxuries we had started with—porridge, jam, butter, marmite, peanut butter, and chocolate—had been eaten long since, and on our arrival, thinking that we should be picked up in a day, we had made pretty free with what was left. We found we could now have ten biscuits each for that day and the next and that the pemmican, tea, sugar, and milk would last the same time. We had nothing else bar one slow-burning carriage candle and so far as we knew the resources of the island were nil. We remembered the solitary hare we had seen and the rifle we had not brought with us. And if *Mischief* had failed to arrive no one at the settlement would even know of our existence. Thus we faced the prospect of starving, with the added refinement of starving within sight of plenty. Obviously before that happened we should have to bestir ourselves. Bruce's air mattress was in good condition—a lash-up of that and driftwood might carry one of us safely across if the sea remained calm.

That night it blew hard from the east and continued blowing next morning. But the sun shone cheerfully as we surveyed the same prospect of wind-swept, sunlit, empty waters, and since cloud hung low over the Baffin Island side we need light no fires nor expect any rescue that day. We moved the tent to a more sheltered hollow and I went for a walk along the beach to the west under the front of the glacier. Bruce seemed sunk in lethargy or was perhaps reserving his strength for a voyage by raft. I can well understand the fascination of beachcombing, especially for a man on an island where the only evidence that there is life elsewhere on this planet is to be found on the beach. I found and discarded all kinds of worthless treasures—the runner of a sledge, a broken oar, whalebones, curious pebbles, the skeleton of a seal. The beach, too, was cluttered with bergy bits cast up by the gale. I took home some sea water which in the absence of salt we were using to flavour the pemmican, and that evening, in the last of our pemmican, we used too much.

Next morning, having made a smoke signal at 8 a.m., we retired to the tent for breakfast. As we were finishing this frugal meal, a mug of tea and three biscuits, thus leaving only seven in the larder, we heard the noise of an engine. In a flash I was outside the tent to see in the distance two small boats. We castaways had no need to wave shirts or light fires to attract their attention. They were obviously heading for our beach and presently two canoes, one large and one small, powered by Johnson outboard engines, landed and out stepped two Eskimos. The man, Kudloo by name, had a smattering of English. A party of Eskimos were apparently camped about five miles west of the Sermilik engaged in hunting seals or perhaps narwhal. They had seen our smoke and had had the sense or the curiosity to come and investigate.

They must have been recently at the settlement because they knew of *Mischief* and they did not need to be told what we wanted.

In no time at all we had packed up, carried the loads to the beach, and dumped them in the big canoe, generously bestowing our remaining biscuits on Kudloo's companion, a young lad. In accord with my sense of fitness these chaps should have come in kayaks, though a kayak would not have helped us much. An umiak would have done—the large skin boat light enough to be carried, formerly used by Eskimos for ice-sea travel, propelled by rudely fashioned oars, while Kudloo and his companion should have been wearing sealskin anoraks and bearskin trousers, reeking emphatically of smoke and blubber. The only concessions Kudloo made towards my ideal were a pair of sealskin boots and a short cutty pipe which remained stuck in his mouth, the bowl close under his nose. The canoes were fine jobs of light plywood construction made in Canada, the big one capable of carrying several tons. The lad had to take the smaller canoe back to their camp. He had also to take with him, though Heaven knows why, some of the ice with which our beach was liberally strewn. I noticed he was choosy about what he took, discarding after a brief glance several pieces that to my inexpert eyes looked like perfectly good ice. This done we all embarked and shot off at a good five knots. When about halfway over both wind and sea got up and I began to think Kudloo might be well advised to turn and run for Bylot Island to await a better day. I pondered, too, how an air mattress would have fared in these conditions. But Kudloo drove on, pipe firmly clenched in his teeth, quite regardless of the spray drenching both himself and his passengers. Soon we sighted a mast and a familiar yellow hull and two hours after leaving we were alongside. Having given Kudloo a well-earned five dollars we climbed on board and surprised the crew still at their breakfast. We thought they looked a bit sheepish.

They had arrived about July 28th, the first ship of the season, followed a week later by the supply ship Bruce and I had seen. During the last few days they had, of course, been looking out for signals and apparently had looked in the right place, but they had seen nothing. With no one now at our camp site to make smoke the matter could not be tested, but Bruce and I had to admit that against the dark background of the moraine our smoke might have gone unnoticed.

Nevertheless we remained secretly convinced that their combined vision, even assisted by binoculars, must be singularly myopic. At any rate all our anxiety had been needless, though we were not to know it. In the course of the next week, seeing no signals, they would have sailed over to look for us. But whether before this happened, Bruce and I, with nothing to eat, would have decided upon a raft, and which of us would have embarked on this dicey voyage, are questions that I am glad we did not have to answer.

Meantime they were full (in every sense) of the hospitality they had received and of the generosity with which the ship had been crammed with food. Apparently we had on board now more food than when we started the voyage. They also told us of their adventures on the passage round, and since these were sometimes exciting I record them here in Ed's own graphic and sometimes telegraphic style:

After Tilman and his party left for the glacier, Mike and myself kept regular ice watch aboard the cutter until the tidal current became weak enough to prevent the floes from moving along the coast. At low water most of them are grounded, some break under their own weight, and the current from our river is then strong enough to carry them seaward. Satisfied that *Mischief* was in no immediate danger we went ashore and erected a stone cairn on the south bank of the river. A rum bottle with the names of the crew, date, and other information was inserted at the base and a board put on top. During the afternoon strong refraction showed on the northern horizon, probably the coast of Devon Island. From the masthead open water showed eastwards.

Later I went ashore to look for the returning party. A lonely, staggering figure of a man carrying an empty rucksack appeared in the distance. Sure enough it was Bob, minus his boots which he had left somewhere and which he wanted Mike to fetch as he was unable to walk, his feet being sore and blistered. We took him on board and he soon fell asleep exhausted by the march. Two hours later Stephen returned. We hove up anchor and left at once under power, for there was no wind. East of Cape Liverpool most of the ice floes were left astern. I tried to signal Tilman's camp by Aldis. No answer. Numerous seals were swimming around. We hoisted the genoa and took it down again; some weak catspaws but not enough to move us. First signs of a steadier breeze came off the bold promontory of Cape Fanshawe when we hoisted all plain sail and stopped the engine. Tacking close inshore among grounded bergs. Possession Bay covered with broken ice and bergy bits. Had we known that Ross's cairn is still there unopened we would have gone in to recover it. Slow progress in light catspaws.

Suddenly after midnight wind shifts NW. in a sudden strong gust which sent us flying southwards. Masthead look-out reports icefloes ahead extending seawards, and more astern. Refraction always makes them look bigger and closer packed than they really are. Towards morning wind dies down and we motor again for a few hours. Passed the floes which are jammed close inshore. Seals everywhere. Ice-fields in bays and inlets along the shore. Heading for Cape Byam Martin. Hoisted genoa and boomed it out with spinnaker pole with a light wind astern. Closing with Cape Graham Moore with snow-clad peaks of Baffin Island clearly visible. Many ice floes at the entrance to Pond Inlet.

Wind freshening as we round the cape 1½ cables off shore. Chart does not show any rocks or soundings so are keeping a sharp lookout in the bows. We gybe to starboard tack and discover some people standing on Button Point. This was Father Roselier and his Eskimo party, as we found out later; they were digging up an old Eskimo settlement. Sky clouding over rapidly with drizzle, and a heavy squall hangs over Albert harbour visible twenty-five miles away. Close shave with huge berg on account Stephen's refusal to steer course as ordered. Wind heading us and we have to sail towards Guys Bight on the Baffin Island side. When in the middle of the sound it falls calm. Drizzle, isolated floes. Current running east, sails down, engine on, heading towards Albert harbour. Mike reports long line of floes ahead. Bloody hell! On closer inspection we manage to get through by long detours. These floes stretch in long unbroken lines at right angles to the current. When closing the land I thought of anchoring in Albert harbour but the crew want to go on.

No wind. Measure fuel in tank and decide to carry on outside Beloeil Island (Albert harbour). Fine clear weather. Doubled the point of Beloeil early in the morning. Mist and fog patches ahead.

Saw Eskimo camp close to rocky shore below Mt Herodier. Saw
more floes ahead, close pack with ice on the water. Motoring more
difficult. Dead slow. Can't manoeuvre. No openings towards Black
Point near Pond Inlet settlement. Turned back and closed the shore
near the Eskimo camp. Motor canoe comes out and Eskimo hunters
come aboard. We sound and drop anchor fifty yards offshore on a
sandy shelf where a strong current eddy keeps driving the menacing ice away. Crew trying to strike bargains in sealskins but no go.
Eskimo want twenty-eight dollars for silver seals. Very fine skins. Old
hunter explains by gestures that the best way to reach the settlement
is by working close inshore.

We sleep for a few hours and early in the afternoon find that
there is a strong movement among the floes. They are driving to the
north so with engine on and lookout at the masthead we manage
to reach Black Point and can see the buildings of the settlement. A
fast motor canoe comes out with two marine biologists, Dr Mansfield
and Tony Welch. They show us an anchorage abreast of the R.C.M.P.
building. Plenty of big floes around moving with east-going current.
As soon as the anchor is down these huge chunks of ice start to move
down on us, fouling the anchor chain and driving us down the bay
despite all our efforts to fend them off. Bob Pilot, the R.C.M.P. corporal in charge of the station, comes out in his uniform with questions and papers*, also some mail for us which came in yesterday
from Frobisher by Canso amphibian. We are the first ship to reach
Pond Inlet this season.

At one moment we are aground. I told Mike to sound. He,
not being familiar with the markings of the lead-line, shouts 'eight
fathoms'. Full astern! Amongst volleys of swearwords and curses
I manage to get her off and decide to go behind Black Point with
Mansfield's canoe sounding ahead of us with an echo-sounder. We
manage to anchor in a narrow place in 2½ fathoms. Current eddy and
rocks off the point keep out most of the floes. Boys went ashore to
walk to the settlement and did not come back until midnight. Next
day a small float-plane landed nearby and was pulled ashore as the ice
situation worsened. [This was a private plane belonging to a young

---

*   It seems a very inopportune moment–H.W.T.

mining magnate who had discovered and was preparing to exploit a
'mountain' of very rich iron ore 200 miles south of Pond Inlet.]

We are now surrounded by closely packed ice. Wind has veered
east pushing floes against our anchor chain, and now and again we
have to start the engine to take the weight off. Met Dr Mansfield
again and agreed to go with them to Ragged Island in Eclipse Sound
about forty miles west of the settlement as soon as the ice cleared. On
every east-going tide there is a great rush of ice through the narrows
towards the open sea and more floes come in from Eclipse Sound.
Bob Pilot gave us a great quantity of food and we moved to the
anchorage off the settlement to load it. The fluke of our main anchor
had been broken off by ice so had to use the CQR anchor which
holds as well or better than the 'fisherman' type. A strong wind from
west helped to clear most of the ice out of Pond Inlet.

We motored out to Ragged Island with Mansfield's whaling
gear and stores on deck. [Dr Mansfield, on behalf of the Canadian
Government, was carrying out research on narwhal which are particularly plentiful in Pond Inlet.] His party in two big canoes caught up
with us off Curry Island. Took several transit bearings to make sure
of our position as the chart is blank and there are two shoals in this
area. Mansfield's transistor echo-sounder was installed in our cockpit as we proceeded towards the north end of Ragged Island, while
his canoe party took the short cut to the south end. Sounded off the
point, a cable distant, and found a sudden shoaling of the water from
no bottom at 200 fathoms to seven fathoms in five minutes. At 1 a.m.
anchored in a bight near the southern point, gravel, three fathoms.
Mansfield's camp on the beach.

Next morning, after setting narwhal nets, two canoes went back
to the Eskimo camp on Curry Island to collect provisions. Some
of the crew went with them taking soundings in the narrow rock-
obstructed passage and finding depths of one fathom. Afterwards
when Mansfield decided to move south towards Eskimo Inlet we
motored back to Pond Inlet, no wind, calm sea. Took some plankton
samples in the area where narwhal blew. Except for a few large bergs
Pond Inlet was now free of ice.

Proceeded to do some deck and maintenance work, but the
crew mostly ashore visiting friends. One night found myself adrift

during strong south-east blow with anchor dragging. Started engine
and motored back to anchorage alone, blowing whistle to attract
attention of crew ashore. All signals useless, as the boys were having
a party in Jack Russell's house. We had a row after they came back.
Next two days devoted to painting and rigging work. Tilman and
Reid arrived in a canoe from Sermilik.

Thus the honour of being the first ship of the season to reach Pond
Inlet, about a week before the regular supply ship arrived, seems to
have been won not without difficulty and danger. I think Ed should
have been presented with a gold cane, like that given to the master
of the first ship to pass up the St Lawrence to Montreal. One judges
from Ed's account that the excitement of arriving at the settlement
and the welcome they received there proved at times too much for the
crew. In rather different circumstances the crews of the old Arctic whalers, when their ship was beset, piled out on the ice, broached the rum,
and generally behaved in what is popularly supposed to be a seamanlike fashion. However, both ship and crew looked in good shape, the
crew in no hurry at all to leave Pond Inlet where they were thoroughly
enjoying themselves. The tiny community had certainly given them a
warm welcome.

CHAPTER VII

HOMEWARD BOUND

POND INLET WAS SO NAMED by John Ross in 1818 after John Pond (1767-1836) who was Astronomer-Royal at that time. That fame is ephemeral is a trite remark but the truth of it is fully borne out in the one small example of Bylot Island. Only a few of the names sprinkled round its coast have been mentioned in this account—Maud Bight, Cape Fanshawe, Cape Byam Martin, Cape Graham Moore, Guys Bight—and who now knows or cares who these men were. None of the residents at Pond Inlet could tell me who Pond was, and I confess it took some trouble on my part to find out.

When we were there the community comprised Corporal Pilot of the R.C.M.P. and his wife; the manager of the Hudson Bay Company's store who, needless to say, was a Scot; the engineer in charge of the power plant; the Roman Catholic padre, the keen ethnologist whom Ed had glimpsed in action at Button Point; and an Anglican padre with his wife and child who had only just arrived in the supply ship. In addition, for the summer only, there were two technicians putting up more buildings, and the two marine biologists enquiring into the narwhal population and its habits. Of the natives of those parts there were some thirty Eskimo families living in tents who, I understood, mostly returned to outlying settlements in the winter. Corporal Pilot exercised control over a large area and in winter spent much of his time touring his domain by dog sledge.

The Hudson Bay Company store was similar to those of the Royal Green and Trading Company along the Greenland coast. Furs, seal-skins, and narwhal horns were bought or exchanged for food, cloth-ing, arms, ammunition, oil, tobacco, etc. We were told that some 1000 sealskins had been bought that season. Thus the Eskimos still live as they have always done by hunting, though nowadays in indirect fash-ion, merely earning money by hunting instead of having to depend on it for food, clothing, and all their necessities. Like most other things the price of sealskins is on the rise. In 1961 at Igdlorssuit in Greenland we had bought average quality skins for £1. In 1963 at Pond Inlet similar skins were worth £5. In the store there were a few narwhal horns from five to seven feet in length. For what purpose the male narwhal uses this formidable implement, no one seems rightly to know. Of two horns still unsold, which I had my eye on, one was imperfect and the other was earmarked as a present for the Governor of the Bank of England. I imagined this financial mogul nonchalantly throwing his silk hat on to it as he clocked in—or, perhaps it would symbolise the horn of plenty.

On the return voyage, instead of sailing the two sides of a triangle by which we had come, we had some hope of steering straight for Godthaab by sailing south-east parallel to the coast of Baffin Island. A signal to 'Ice Control Halifax' asking about the ice conditions and for advice as to our best route, brought a very detailed ice report and a recommendation to take the northern route as we had done on the way up. The Middle Pack had receded southwards a little but near the Canadian coast the ice remained too thick for us to navigate. It seems easier to get a report on ice conditions in the Canadian Arctic than for the coasts of Greenland.

In return for the kindness we had received, before leaving we had a party on board. Those of our guests for whom there was room had scarcely got themselves below before the party was diminished by two. The slight motion of the boat at anchor proved too much for Mrs Pilot who had to be taken hurriedly ashore by her husband. Later we were joined by the mining magnate and his pilot who touched down almost alongside in their small plane, and by the narwhal research party. The latter told us that they had netted fifteen narwhal in the narrows off Ragged Island, one with an eight-foot horn.

After making our farewells ashore we sailed out on the morning of August 15th with a very light wind. The deck and hull had been painted, we had filled up with oil at a cost of only twenty-eight dollars with a drum of furnace oil thrown in; and we had on board enough food for several months, much of it of a kind that _Mischief's_ crews seldom see. An austere sufficiency is usually their portion. We had eggs in the shell, bacon, huge tins of ham, pickles, fancy biscuits, tins of lime juice and orange juice, meats and soups in bewildering variety, fishcakes, olives, salted peanuts, jams, honey, and maple syrup. I have long been of the opinion that all tinned foods taste much the same after the initial impact of surprise or disgust has worn off. At sea in a small boat, where tinned food is for the most part inevitable, there is no remedy for this dull uniformity except to carry enough onions, garlic, and above all Tabasco sauce. All this variety simplified Bob's problems, the crew having so much scope for browsing that the main meals hardly mattered.

On our way out we passed inside Beloeil Island in order to examine Albert harbour, before sailing slowly down the inlet on a lovely evening, the snows of Bylot Island bathed in sunshine. For two days the sea remained so void of ice that we began edging south a little too soon. In Lat. 72° 44′ we saw ice to the south and at midnight of the 17th we found ourselves in fog amongst floes. At 1 a.m. I went below thinking we were clear, leaving Ed and Bruce on deck. The continuous uproar that ensued as they repeatedly went about to avoid more floes was more than I could stand, so we hove to rather precariously with floes on all sides. We should, I suppose, have had the sails down but by leaving them up we could steer clear of any threatening floe merely by letting draw. Finally Mike contrived to lay us smartly alongside a big floe and the wind in the sail defied all our efforts to part company with it. Down the sail had to come and with the engine in reverse we got off with no harm but loss of paint.

This tendency to edge southwards had to be suppressed. We motored due north through scattered floes with solid pack still to the east until by evening we were able to start sailing. Our wire rigging was covered with verglas such as the luckless climber sometimes finds on rock, the air temperature being 34° and the sea 35°. Next morning we were again wrapped in a clammy blanket of fog. When at length the sun shone on an empty sea we began sailing south-east until a distant fog bank and the low growling of pack-ice once more warned us away.

The danger that one can see is much less fearful than the unseen danger. The nights had now begun to get dark so that we were much relieved when by August 20th we had seen the last of ice and icebergs. We passed some ninety miles west of Upernivik and sighted the Greenland coast first in the neighbourhood of Disko Island. Several

Portuguese schooners were still busy filling their holds with salt cod. On the Hellefiske Bank we saw a four-master and later sailed through a fleet of dories. A falling glass and a rising wind heralded a long spell of dirty weather as we closed the land north of Godthaab. Having picked up the beacon on the outer islands we sailed up the fjord and gained the harbour as the wind rose to gale force. Even the prospect of beer at the Kristinemut failed to persuade us to venture ashore on that wet and windy night.

Despite continuous rain next day we were all ashore shopping, stocking up with bread, and making arrangements through our Canadian friend for the return by air of Nissen's rifle. When we went alongside for paraffin and water on the 29th the air was damp, muggy, and still. The calm before the storm, as we might have guessed, for no sooner had we cleared the harbour than it began blowing hard from south. With the wind in that quarter we should do no good, but rather than put back into Godthaab we took shelter in the lee of an island on the south side of the fjord. All that night, the next day, and the following night, while the glass fell to 29.2, the rain drummed incessantly on the deck and the waters of the fjord were whipped into foam. The man on anchor watch amused himself by catching cod. When the wind at last veered and moderated we beat out past the islands in a heavy swell. As we took our departure from the last island we were able once more to stream our log, having now collected the new rotator that we had ordered from England upon first arriving at Godthaab.

The sails and ropes that had been sodden for a week had just begun to dry out when late that night another gale hit us from southeast, the glass again falling to 29.2. Unluckily we were still within reach of the Godthaab weather forecasts; or at least Ed could listen to them because he was the only one who had any Danish. Besides experiencing our own bad weather we suffered vicariously as Ed recounted for our benefit all the gales then howling round the coasts of Greenland, including a monstrous one of Force 10 off Cape Farewell. This, he assured us, would inevitably move in our direction. In fact for the next six days we enjoyed reasonably pleasant weather for the time of year, and withal managed to put so many miles between ourselves and the Voice of Godthaab that its croaking could no longer be heard. At this period we enjoyed many very beautiful nights. Even the moon at full failed to dim the splendour of the aurora as it flung vast glowing arches across the sky or draped it with shimmering curtains of pale, green pulsating light.

By September 7th we were already sixty miles south of Cape Farewell, the weather raw and drizzly, and no wind until nightfall when we began a fast run under twin staysails. On the two previous homeward voyages in September the weather had been no worse than in June which is reckoned the quietest month in the Atlantic. According to statistics, however, more gales can be expected. And, of course, everyone assumes he will be blown out of his bed or bunk round about the equinox, September 20th. Lecky, however, who even if old-fashioned can be accepted as an oracle in all sea-faring matters, holds that there are no such things as 'equinoctial gales'. 'Equinoctial gales', he writes, 'constitute one of those prejudices of which it is well-nigh hopeless to disabuse the popular mind. Most careful observations prove conclusively that storms have no special connection with the equinoxes; yet how often does one hear a gale, occurring even three weeks one side or other of this event referred to as an equinoctial gale.'

On September 11th, when we were some 360 miles west of Cape Farewell, after rolling becalmed throughout the morning watch, by afternoon we were hove-to with a forty-knot wind from south-west. We had the storm jib up and gradually increased the number of rolls in the mainsail until only about five feet of the luff remained hoisted. She lay quietly enough, forereaching crabwise at nearly two knots. By midnight the wind had moderated and veered. We started sailing and by noon next day were doing six and a half knots, a speed at which *Mischief* begins to tremble with excitement. In fact we had another gale at our backs and when a great dollop of water fell in the cockpit we took the hint, handed the sails, and let her run. At dusk we ventured to hoist the staysail but soon had it down again, the wind increasing throughout the night.

When I came on watch at 4 a.m., an hour when a man is very easily impressed, when the size of the seas hissing by begins to be dimly discernible in the murky light of dawn, I rated the stronger gusts at Force 10. Towards the end of my watch another wave flooded the cockpit and its unhappy occupant. Most of this water found its

way below thus rousing Ed who thought the time had come to stream
a drogue to slow us down.

Ed had recently renewed the canvas of the drogue but not the
roping. Certainly its launching over the stern appeared to quieten her
down. We were all delighted, especially Ed, until half an hour later,
when we gave the warp a tug and discovered that the drogue was no
longer at the other end. I believe it had parted almost as soon as we
streamed it. This violent depression, a secondary following that of the
previous day, soon passed. But Ed did his best to diminish the satisfaction that its passing afforded us by predicting that such weather
might last from September to March, though, of course, we hoped to
be home before then. Things below were becoming a bit damp, particularly my bunk which is the most vulnerable on account of having
no other bunk above it.

For the next two days, reefed and in thick weather, we tramped
along at the rate of over 100 miles a day. We met a ship, the *Manchester Merchant*, which came close to have a good look at us but did not
reply to our lamp signals. When approaching Ireland in poor visibility
we were on the wrong tack to clear it, the wind being south-east. We
could not have made so free with the desolate coasts we had recently
quitted where there are no warnings for the mariner. Soon, out on the
starboard bow, we heard the friendly bellowing of the Bull lighthouse.
There is quite a farmyard off this south-west corner of Ireland. Bull
Island, off Dursey Head, had for its immediate neighbours the Cow,
Calf, and Heifer, not to mention the Cat or Crow rocks.

Thanks to Ed's devoted attention our battery had remained fully
charged. We did not have to sup by candle-light and perforce observe
wireless silence as had usually been the case at the latter end of a
voyage. Naturally gale warnings began flowing in. Certainly in the
last days of the passage from September 20th to September 25th we
had a lot of wind—the equinoctial gales as, no doubt, the uninstructed
would think? All day of the 25th and the succeeding night, when we
had been told to expect that the violent north-west wind then blowing would back south-west, we carried on for the Scillies on the port
tack. When we had overshot the Bishop by some forty miles the wind
did at last go round and blew to such purpose that forty hours later we
passed the Needles, twenty-six days out from Godthaab and a record

passage. In 1961 it had taken us twenty-nine days and in 1962 no less than thirty-four.

Happily after all this wind and rain, both the day of our arrival and the next day were fine enough for us to dry the sails and to strip *Mischief* bare ready for laying up. It was time for our small self-contained community to part. After so many days at sea together between water and sky the crew went their several ways—Ed to a merchant ship, Bruce to train with the R.A.F., Stephen to learn farming, and Mike to Australia. Bob disappeared as mysteriously as he had come and I have not heard of him since. We had made our voyage, as the saying goes, had achieved what we had set out to do. I felt we had been lucky. There is no water anywhere that is foolproof, and northern waters are less so than the average.

PART TWO

East Greenland
Mischief

May–September, 1964

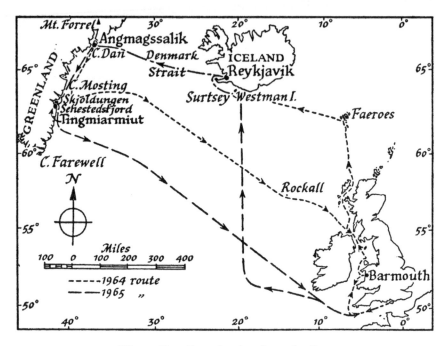

Map 3: East Greenland, 1964 and 1965

CHAPTER VIII

THE OBJECTIVE AND THE CREW

◆

Nothing lasts like the provisional. When I bought *Mischief* in 1954 for a voyage to the Patagonian channels for a specific purpose I did not expect her to last many years, or that I should have the opportunity to go on sailing her year after year until our lives, so to speak, had become intertwined. But as the years went by, the ship showing less sign of wear than her owner, I came to believe that she would last my time. During the winter of 1963–1964, however, our partnership very nearly came to an end. When cleaning up below in the cabin on our return in September, we found some rot in the lining of the cabin. So before leaving *Mischief* to enjoy her hard-earned winter's repose in the mud berth that she has occupied since she first came to Lymington in November 1954, I asked the yard to take out the plank lining and replace it with peg-board which would allow more ventilation. In old boats it is generally the case that the more you stir the more it stinks, the removal of one bit of wood leading to the discovery of further horrors. On removing the lining it was found that many of the oak frames were in places soft, in other words rotten; there was plenty of sound wood in the frames but it meant that some of the fastenings, on which everything depends, could not be trusted to hold.

According to the Persian proverb, 'the wise man sits on the hole in his carpet.' This plan is not really applicable to faults in boats, at least not in a boat that you wish to sail yourself. So before long I returned to the boatyard and went on board together with a friend who was also a surveyor. The interior of a boat out of commission in winter is never a cheerful scene, and *Mischief*'s cold, dank cabin, condensation dripping from the beams, looked the worse for having apparently suffered at the hands of wreckers. It reeked of desolation, decay, death, and as the surveyor began methodically prodding the frames with a thin spike I sensed his face growing longer at every prod.

In his opinion the old boat—not quite sixty years old—which had carried me and my crews for so many thousands of miles had, so to speak, had it. She had reached the end of her tether so far as deep water voyages were concerned though she might be good for several more years of pottering round the coast. He strongly advised me against allowing myself to be talked into spending more money on her, even the expense of having her hauled out for a proper survey would not be justified. This was bitter medicine.

> The first bringer of unwelcome news
> Hath but a losing office; and his tongue
> Sounds ever after as a sullen bell
> Remembered tolling a departed friend.

Nothing has an uglier look than reason when it is not of our side. Sentiment is no good guide for action, but the old boat had come to mean a lot to me and when I looked at her lying there, to all appearances as stout as ever, I could not bring myself to write her off then and there as one might an old car. A second opinion is usually asked for in the hope rather than the belief that it will contradict the first. Nevertheless before coming to a decision I had another surveyor to look at her after she had undergone further stripping inside. The verdict was the same: 'She is no longer fit for the sort of use you require—extended cruising—though she could still give several years service for inshore sailing where she is unlikely to be subjected to prolonged heavy weather stresses.'

What to do with her was then the question. Apart from the fact that it was not what I wanted, I did not think that short cruises would repay the expense of fitting out or the trouble of finding fresh crews every season. Nor did I want to sell her, to hear of her later rotting away neglected, or ending her days ignominiously as a houseboat. Perhaps someone could be found who would be interested in preserving her as an example of a Bristol Channel pilot cutter. Apart from models, and with the notable and magnificent exception of Cutty Sark, nowhere are there preserved any relics of the days of sail, any examples of the various types of fishing and working boats that even fifty years ago could be found round our coasts. By now it is probably too late. As it happened I had to spend the inside of a week in America that winter to attend a climbing reunion. I took the chance of having a look at Old Mystic, formerly a Connecticut whaling port, which is being refashioned as it once was, complete with rope-walk, sail-loft, smithy, and the rest. Lying in the harbour they have the old whaling ship William Morgan, the barque Joseph Conrad, a big schooner yacht noted for several Arctic voyages, and a number of lesser craft. Another maritime museum I visited at Newport News also had several original examples of sailing vessels. In America there are plenty of wealthy men to endow such places and I understood that in these two instances the interest shown by the public makes them almost self-supporting.

In Janury I began the search for another old or oldish boat to replace *Mischief*, having in the meantime received some enquiries about her future from people interested in encouraging boys to sail. On the way down to the west country to look at a boat I stopped at Lymington and naturally paid a visit to *Mischief* looking, I thought, most forlorn and disconsolate in her mud berth. That time and chance play a greater part in arranging our future than we would care to admit has been noted before by even less penetrating minds than mine. When chance intervenes to change one's plans—as it was about to do to mine—one is almost persuaded that history itself is a chapter of accidents, or is even willing to accept the degrading notion that our world is merely the result of a 'fortuitous concourse of atoms'.

Chance meetings in pubs seldom lead to much good. But it was such a meeting that led ultimately to giving *Mischief* a further lease of life. In *The Ship* I got talking to Wing Commander R. H. A. Coombes whom, by the way, except for brief greetings in the boatyard, I had not met before. He listened to my dismal tale with an understanding ear, for he was then engaged in refitting, almost rebuilding *Isoletta*, a seventy-foot ketch built in 1909, having bought the bare hull cheap. He took a robust view of *Mischief*'s troubles and recommended having her hauled out and properly examined. He was confident that she would be found sound enough below the water-line, in which case the upper frames could very well be made good by doubling up. This was the sort of advice I wanted to hear and it was therefore quickly accepted, thus contradicting Dr Johnson's dictum that 'Few things are so liberally bestowed, or squandered with so little effect, as good advice.' Besides advice I had absorbed a few pints. Doubly fortified I went straight back to the yard and made arrangements to have *Mischief* hauled out for inspection.

The result answered expectations. The timbers below the water-line were sound enough and by doubling the upper parts of the frames she could be made seaworthy. Obviously it was not going to be cheap but it would be less expensive than buying another boat, especially an old boat with which one might also buy trouble. I had, too, some misgivings at flying in the face of professional advice and, perhaps, at allowing myself to be too much influenced by sentiment. In the end I decided to have the work done.

Once this piece of folly, as some would call it, had been committed, I began thinking of committing another that coming summer. Instead of making a fourth voyage to the west coast of Greenland I thought of visiting the east coast, a place that hitherto I had regarded as unsuitable for a small boat. One authority is emphatic on this point:

> East Greenland has much more pack-ice than West Greenland and no ship should attempt to navigate in its waters unless it is specially designed. The east Greenland ice is usually broken and rafted into heavy floes of various sizes often with a thickness of twenty to thirty feet. It is too great to cut with the prow of a ship. The ice-belt is traversed by seeking out the leads of open water, thus the course is tortuous, the ship twisting and turning, worming its way between the floes and fields. A high premium is placed on short turning circles and the manoeuvrability of vessels such as the Norwegian seal-hunter type. Experienced navigators on meeting the ice-edge off north-east Greenland are said to insist on clear weather and a steady barometer before attempting passage to the coast.

Although the foregoing is certainly true it refers chiefly to the more northern part of that coast. A study of the ice-charts for the months of July and August showed that there was not much ice on the coast south of Lat. 63°. As the *Arctic Pilot* says:

> Throughout the period December to June inclusive the ice along the entire length of the coast from Lat. 80° to Cape Farewell (Lat. 60°) is wholly impenetrable. With the advance of summer the pack becomes

lighter and more open along the southern part of the coast, particularly from the region of Scoresby Sund (Lat. 70°) southward. In an
average year, the ice in this region is mainly navigable by ordinary
vessels in August to October inclusive; along the most southern part
of the coast from Lat. 64° to Cape Farewell there are large stretches
of open water in September and October. In July from Lat. 61° to
Cape Farewell the ice is mainly navigable, but patches of unnavigable ice may be met.

Thus if one kept south of Lat. 64° there seemed to be a fair chance of
reaching the coast. This coast, like the west coast, is fringed with islets
and islands and, in the south, by a narrow strip of ice-free land. It is
likewise much indented with fjords—an arm of Scoresby Sund forms
the longest fjord in the world. Life of any kind is more scarce than on
the west coast. Its mountains are higher. Mt Watkins (12,139 feet) is the
highest mountain in Greenland and further south is Mt Forrel (11,024
feet). There are only two trading stations on the coast, at Scoresby
Sund and at Angmagssalik (Lat. 65° 36′). Since the war, an increasing number of mountaineering parties have visited the regions of the
higher mountains, usually going by air from Iceland to Scoresby Sund
or Angmagssalik.

South of Angmagssalik, the only part of the coast that we could
expect to reach in *Mischief*, the mountains are of the order of 4000 to
6000 feet, quite high enough for me. The place I picked on after reading the *Pilot* and studying the chart was Skjoldungen (Lat. 63°) where
two fjords, North and South Skjoldungen, run inland for about twenty-
five miles where they are joined together by a deep channel. The mountainous island of Skjoldungen lying between the two fjords seemed a
fascinating bit of little-known country. The *Pilot* noted that a valley at
the head of South Skjoldungen contains a good salmon river and has
a comparatively rich vegetation; but my main reason for choosing this
fjord was because in it there is no great glacier descending from the ice
cap to clutter it up with floes and bergs as is the case in many of the
East Greenland fjords.

Whether or not we called first at Angmagssalik depended to some
extent upon ice conditions. It would be the correct thing to do in
order to make ourselves known to the Greenland authorities. In any

case it would be little use to arrive off the coast before the latter half of
July, so that if we started at the usual time at the end of May we should
have time to visit both the Faeroes and Iceland. Making a rough plan
is easier than finding a crew to assist in carrying it out. Experience
had shown that I need not try to collect a crew of seasoned yachtsmen or even a nucleus of such. There is less in this than meets the eye,
as Talulah Bankhead remarked. It was not so much that experienced
hands knew better than to embark in *Mischief*, but rather that such
men either sail their own boats or crew for their friends. My recruits
are found mainly among young chaps with a taste for adventure who
have not yet settled down or have settled down prematurely in a job
not to their liking. If they have any qualifications so much the better,
but if not it is no great matter. It is unfortunate from my point of
view that none of these young men ever have any money to contribute
towards the expenses. On the other hand, if they did contribute they
might feel themselves entitled to make suggestions or even to complain, like passengers who have paid their fare. As the Chinese say,
quietness is worth buying.

Having before had some contact with Bangor University I had two
recruits from that source. Roger Coward, a history student in his last
year, was not entirely inexperienced having sailed racing dinghies. He
was keen to make a film and in a position to borrow a 16-mm camera
provided I would supply the film. In spite of having done this before
and found it not repaying, I agreed. Besides the cost of the film, the
shooting of it involves a certain amount of pain. It would be an exag-
geration to say that if a man fell overboard the camera man would ask
him to do it again slowly, but all the more usual activities on board
have to be rehearsed for his benefit or done when there is no occasion to do them. The other Bangor representative was Charles Sewell, a
young laboratory assistant and an active rock climber. Bangor University, having at its doorstep the Menai Straits for sailing and Snowdonia
for climbing, should have a high proportion of sane undergraduates—
and professors, too, for that matter.

M. Wareham was a young engineer apprentice at the Berthon Boatyard, Lymington, thus well acquainted with boats and with *Mischief*.
Although barely eighteen he was a useful acquisition. He was generally
known as 'Noddy' from his habit of wearing a wool cap with a bob on

it perched precariously on a mat of curly, copper hair. This particular cap soon went overboard.

L. D. R. Cook had spent some years in a R.A.F. Mountain Rescue team in Scotland where he had acquired an interest in climbing. His size and weight made up for the lack of brawn in the others who were mostly lightweights. He had enjoyed what one assumes must be only a spasmodically active life in the Mountain Rescue team but was nonetheless evidently a misfit in the R.A.F. with a strong dislike for authority and 'bull'—a common attitude of present day youth, admirable only up to a point. At this time he was employed in London as store accountant by a firm importing French cosmetics, though what Bob Cook could have in common with French cosmetics is almost beyond conjecture.

Finally I got hold of an old friend Major E. H. Marriott. The initials must be some sort of under-cover address to fox the enemy for I have never heard him referred to as anything else but Charles. He had sailed with me on a voyage to the Patagonia channels as a climber, and on the first Greenland voyage when he both cooked and climbed. Thus he was now to make a third voyage in *Mischief*, a triumph, some might say, of hope over experience. We already had two climbers on board, three including myself, and since Charles Marriott at that time was not over-fit he was prepared to forego any mountaineering. He agreed to come as cook, a role that is exacting and always difficult to fill. It requires a strong stomach, the balance and agility of a juggler; indifference to being sprayed with cold sea water from the galley hatch and very hot water from the stove; the ability to work in a confined space breathing rather foul air; and the same energy, patience, and goodwill as that needed by a hen cormorant to sustain her mouth-gaping offspring. All these Charles had to some extent, particularly the first and the last. Besides this he was an experienced hand who in the first few trying days of the voyage could take a watch and help to show the greenhorns how things should be done. He was also good company if you like the company of a chap who will argue any point or no point, and he had a fund of anecdotes and doubtful stories. Some of these would be new to the crew, and even to me who had been with him twelve months on the first occasion and four on the second, for I have a very short memory.

CHAPTER IX

TO THE FAEROE ISLANDS

THE EXTENSIVE REPAIRS to *Mischief*'s ribs having been completed the crew began to assemble from May 20th onwards. One or two of them I had met only once before for a few brief moments, so that when they stepped on board, instead of a welcoming smile, my face must have worn a look of shocked surprise. Had I or had I not met this chap before somewhere? Surely I had not asked him to come? The lean, wiry Charles Sewell bore a horrible resemblance to someone I had sailed with many years before and when he upset the varnish tin twice the first day this fear was almost confirmed. Charles Marriott ran true to form by deferring his arrival from day to day and consequently our departure. It did not matter. Rain delayed the fitting out and for two days I myself felt more like going to bed than going to sea.

Our wireless set, a type that is fitted in motor cars, had at last succumbed to sea-air and damp. I invested in a Decca transistor set, supposed to give world-wide coverage, so that we need no longer depend upon the battery and the charging engine. With a good chronometer watch a wireless receiving set is not essential. Watches, however, have been known to stop, especially if one forgets to wind them, and if Test Matches are being played a reliable receiving set is important. Weather forecasts can be obtained only for home waters and need not necessarily be taken too much to heart. West of the areas Shannon and Rockall forecasts for the Atlantic are transmitted in Morse too fast for the average yachtsman, while those for Iceland or Greenland waters will be in some unknown tongue.

Charles Marriott arrived on May 30th at 11.30 and we cast off at 12.30 after a hurried lunch. As we motored down the river the Royal Lymington Yacht Club honoured us with a salute from their starting gun. With the ebb tide and a light wind we soon cleared the Needles, but in the evening a violent squall ushered in a night of torrential rain, thunder, lightning, and squalls from all points of the compass.

Not at all the sort of night to be at sea with a green crew. We had several Chinese gybes, were scared by steamers, and enjoyed five minutes' pandemonium when the staysail sheet got out of control. The next night was a repetition of the first, worse in fact, for Charles Marriott lost overboard his yachting cap, a veteran of many voyages, at least ten years old to my knowledge, much prized by him and greatly admired by the crew. No longer would a slimmer edition of King Edward VII be seen disembarking from *Mischief* as though from the royal yacht *Britannia*.

By June 1st the weather had faired up and the wind died down to leave us rolling heavily. A corvette steamed slowly past and hailed us by name to know if we were all right. The crew, discomfited by the heavy rolling, might not have agreed with my affirmative reply. We discovered now that the metal collar for the twin staysail booms had been left behind, like the proverbial Dutchman's anchor. It was infuriating to have the sails on board and no means of setting them. Our course down Channel had no doubt been tortuous. On June 2nd the visibility being poor, I reckoned we must be somewhere near the Manacles. But life is full of surprises. When the wind fell light we handed the mainsail in order to stitch a seam and while I was busy with this Noddy sighted through the haze a slender tower to the north-east—no doubt, the Eddystone. But when the sun went down and the lights came on it proved to be the Wolf Rock light. We were at least twenty miles and two points out in our reckoning. I concluded that *Mischief* knew the way down Channel better than her skipper.

Astonishment is an emotion salutary for the young—and the old, too, for that matter. Presently we were to have even greater cause than this for astonishment, and these two strange occurrences went far to confirm my belief that navigation is far from being an exact science. Bound for East Greenland via the Faeroes and Iceland our best course lay up the Irish Sea and through the Minches. Upon rounding Land's End, therefore, we set a course for the Smalls. Thick weather obliged us to go about before sighting them but on the evening of June 4th we had the Tuskar rock abeam five miles off. Taking our departure from this unmistakable mark we set a course for Holyhead eighty miles away, a course that enabled us to make the most of a fine quartering wind. The wind held steady all night and next day, which was hazy, we were puzzled but not dismayed when we found we had run 100 miles without either hitting or even sighting Holyhead Island. At last about tea-time, when land began to loom vaguely to port, to starboard, and also ahead, we realised that we were near the head of Cardigan Bay, two points off course and some forty miles from Holyhead. Currents, the compass, the helmsmen, even the navigator, may be responsible for these anomalies. It is not, however, for the navigator to accept responsibility for them or to show surprise, or he may sap what confidence the crew have in him. Attack is the best form of defence. A few remarks about the impossibility of navigating the ship if it is not steered straight will restore his own confidence and subdue and mystify the crew.

> Where lies the land to which the ship will go?
> Far, far ahead is all her seamen know.
> And where the land she travels from? Away
> Far, far behind is all that they can say.

The tide being foul we went outside Bardsey Island and headed across to Ireland, the wind by now round at north. In poor visibility we were lucky to sight St John's lighthouse whence we set a course to clear South Rock, the most easterly point of Ireland. The night closed down dark and foggy and we were sailing fast, so mindful of recent events I prudently decided to heave to. Several ships were about with their foghorns blaring and before dawn we received aid and comfort by hearing away on our beam the bleating of Mew Island lighthouse south of Belfast Lough. Approaching the North Channel on a clear, sunny evening, the wind light, we had the doubtful pleasure of watching the Stranraer-Larne ferry cross and recross no less than four times. Here the tides run strongly and, perhaps, I had not been explicit enough about the course to steer if the wind freshened. Coming on deck early next morning I found we were up behind the Mull of Kintyre, none of the helmsmen in the night having realised that he was steering blithely into a cul-de-sac. By the time we had regained the North Channel, and once more sighted the ferryboat, the tide had turned against us, leaving us no choice but to steer west for Red Bay and anchor there.

Leaving on the north-going tide, by 1 p.m. of June 9th we had Inishtrahull abeam, whence we set a course for Skerryvore. Inishtrahull and Skerryvore! What stirring, romantic names for the two lonely, Atlantic-facing outposts of Ireland and Scotland ! Skerryvore is one of a shoal of above-water and sunken rocks extending for twelve miles to the south of the Isle of Tiree. It must be a fearsome sight in a gale when the whole of this twelve miles is a mass of breakers. The lighthouse, designed by Alan Stevenson and finished in 1844, must be one of the most exposed of any, wide open as it is to the unbroken sweep of the Atlantic.

After passing Skerryvore we had a grand sail through the Passage of Tiree, the five-miles-wide strait between Mull and the two bleak, barren islands of Tiree and Coll. Johnson and Boswell in their tour of the Hebrides were driven by a storm to take refuge in Coll where they remained weatherbound for nearly a fortnight:

> We were doomed to experience, like others, the dangers of trusting to the wind, which blew against us in a short time with such violence that we, being so seasoned sailors, were willing to call it a tempest. I was sea-sick and lay down. Mr Boswell kept the deck. The master knew not well whither to go; and our difficulties might well have filled a very pathetic page, had not Maclean of Coll, who with every other qualification that insular life requires is a very active and skilful mariner, piloted us safe into his own harbour.

Boswell devotes several pages to this adventure of which the following is a brief sample:

> ... a prodigious sea with immense billows coming upon the vessel so that it seemed hardly possible to escape. There was something grandly horrible in the sight ... As I saw them all busy doing something, I asked Coll what I could do. He, with a happy readiness, put into my hand a rope, which was fixed to the top of one of the masts, and told me to hold it till he bade me pull. If I had considered the matter I might have seen that this could not be of the least service but his object was to keep me out of the way of those who were busy working the vessel, and at the same time divert my fear by employing

me, and making me think I was of use. Thus did I stand firm to my post while the wind and rain beat upon me, always expecting a call to pull my rope.

From what we saw of Coll and its small harbour as we sailed by I think Boswell had good reason to be afraid, running as they were for a small, unlit harbour, in a gale, on a black night. Among the Hebrides with their strong tides, strong winds, and much rain, the perils of navigation when there were no harbour lights or lighthouses are hardly imaginable. Nowadays, in summer at least, there are no difficulties thanks to the numerous lights. Rounding the north end of Coll we stood across to Ushinish lighthouse on South Uist passing on the way the rocks of Oigh Sgeir where there is also a light. From Ushinish we made for the Little Minch at the north end of Skye, faithfully following the pecked line on the chart, the recommended route for north-bound vessels, like a hen following a chalk-line. Once through the pass of the Little Minch we were in the clear, for the North Minch is over thirty miles wide.

It seemed a shame to pass non-stop through this perfect cruising ground with only the vaguest glimpse of the mountains of Skye. These western isles were no more familiar to the crew than Greenland but at this stage of the voyage they were more interested in sleep than in scenery. On the evening of June 11th we passed the Butt of Lewis and sailed out into the Atlantic. The Faeroes lie due north, only 180 miles away, with nothing in between but the small uninhabited islands of Sula Sgeir and Rona. We sighted the former on the 12th; it is visited in summer by people from Lewis to collect the eggs of the gannet or solan goose. A mixture of rain and fog, flat calms and high winds, made this short passage slow and uncertain. I got no sun sights, only a sight of Vega, and one star by itself is not of great value. Sailing north in summer the nights soon become so light that only planets or the very brightest stars are visible—visible, that is to say, to the navigator with a sextant that is a little antique like mine, with a telescope that hinders rather than helps the picking up of stars. Even when the nights are dark the North Atlantic sky, after remaining clear all night, has a mean trick of clouding over before dawn when one is hoping to take star sights. The exasperated navigator then feels like echoing the impious outburst ascribed to Lord Jeffrey, a contemporary of Sydney Smith, though what circumstances occasioned the outburst I have not discovered: 'Damn the solar system; bad light; planets too distant; pestered with comets; feeble contrivance; could make a better with ease.'

After remaining hove to most of the night in a near gale and heavy rain, still uncertain of our position, we let draw on the morning of the 14th, steering east. Two trawlers were in sight and at noon a high island showed up on the starboard bow some twenty miles away. It could be only Syderö the southernmost of the Faeroes. There are altogether eighteen islands, all but one inhabited, spread over about sixty miles of sea. There are many good harbours, a few of them classed as 'winter harbours' safe in all weather conditions, and the rest are 'summer harbours'. My only knowledge of the Faeroes, strictly practical, came from the *Pilot*; we did not know where to find the choicest beauty spots or the cheapest beer; even Charles Marriott, a rich storehouse of general knowledge, was at a loss. I inclined to the capital, Thorshaven, or Vaag Fjord on Syderö, both on the east side of the group and therefore sheltered.

Three miles off the south end of Syderö is a thirty-seven-foot-high rock called Munken and in the vicinity of the rock there are heavy tide rips even in fine weather. That evening we were sailing eastwards about two miles south of Munken, thinking that was enough. Apparently it was not. The wind dropped and almost at once the sea, as if glad to be free of its control, began to boil like a pot. All around us waves shot up and collapsed in confusion. As we had no steerage way the sails and spars slammed and banged, the mast quivered. Broken water extended as far as the eye could reach. We were being set westwards anyway, so we forgot about Thorshaven and Vaag Fjord, started the engine, and steered north-west, intent only on getting out of this miniature maelstrom.

When we were well west of Syderö conditions improved except for a heavy swell running and an absence of wind. We handed all sails except the genoa which we stupidly left up with the result that it split right across. But we had by no means finished with our Faeroe Island troubles. Our best bet now seemed to be Vestmanhavn in Vestmanha Sund, the narrow channel between the main island Stromo and the westernmost island Vaago. From there, to continue our voyage to

Iceland, we should merely have to complete the passage of the Sund to fetch clear of the islands and be out in the Atlantic. Entering Vestmanhavn we should have to fly a 'Q' flag which we now discovered we had also left behind. So while waiting for a wind I made up a flag with canvas and curry powder.

Towards noon a breeze came in from west enabling us just to lay the desired course. All seemed set fair for a quick passage to Vaago Fjord followed by a quiet night at anchor in Vestmanhavn. In the afternoon, however, the weather deteriorated, squalls of wind and rain became gradually heavier and more frequent, blotting out all the land except for two 1500-foot-high islands close on our starboard hand. Prudence suggested reefing or even standing out to sea for the night, for the wind had in it a note of malice and we were on a lee shore in thick weather. But without the driving power of the full mainsail we should never clear Kolter, the northermost of the two islands now fine on the lee bow. With Vaago Fjord and its promise of shelter only five miles away we drove on under all plain sail, the lee scuppers awash, praying that the gear would stand and that we could weather Kolter. As if to enhance the wild, adventurous aspect of the scene—the hard-driven ship, the angry sea, the dim, menacing outline of the island—a blue whale, close aboard, jumped half clear of the water, fell back with a splash that could be heard above the roar of the wind, and then towered, head and shoulders clear of the water, before sounding.

With Kolter gradually drawing safely aft we could turn our attention to what lay ahead, peering through the gathering gloom of rain and nightfall in search of the fjord entrance. Between the heavier curtains of rain that swept across we made out the black outline of an immense vertical wall of rock fine on the weather bow. For this we steered, certain that it would provide us with a lee and trusting that it marked the entrance to the fjord. In the smooth water in the lee of this precipice we got the sails off, for the wind now whistled straight down the fjord which lay directly ahead. Vestmanhavn is some eight miles up the fjord and we had not gone more than a couple of miles, motoring into the teeth of the blast, when we began to have doubts about reaching it. Either the wind had increased or the tide turned against us, for we almost stood still. There was no anchoring anywhere in this wall-sided fjord so once more we abandoned our immediate objective, turned tail, and shot back down the fjord.

About three miles west of the fjord entrance and the great cliff which we now knew was Stakken there is a small harbour called Midvaag. Although it was on the weather side of Stakken we hoped that by creeping close along the shore we could cheat the wind and find moderately smooth water. As we rounded close under Stakken we regarded with awe its lesser but more extraordinary neighbour, a detached pinnacle like a gigantic Napes Needle, over 1000 feet high, called Troldkonefinger. Bucking the wind and sea, our speed reduced to a crawl, we watched the rocks close inshore anxiously as we crept slowly by. Soon we were in more sheltered water and at last at midnight we let go in three fathoms between some fishing craft and a small breakwater. There had been no time for supper in the stress and strain of the last few hours. Before turning in Charles dished up soup, bully, and spuds, alleviating this austerity with cocoa and rum. Midvaag is not a 'winter harbour' and since the wind and rain continued unabated we set an anchor watch.

CHAPTER X

SURTSEY AND REYKJAVIK

IT IS FUN TO ARRIVE BY NIGHT at a strange harbour, wondering what daylight will reveal—unless it happens to be one of those busy ports where one may well be knocked up long before daylight to be told that you have anchored in the fairway or a prohibited area. From our short acquaintance with the Faeroes and the seas around, the tide-rips, the cliffs, and the grey clouds covering them, we did not expect much in the way of habitation. But any place that has afforded the seafarer shelter on a stormy night is bound to be regarded with kindly eyes.

No doubt on a wet, windy morning Midvaag was not looking its best, but the line of white cottages nestling below the green hillside where a few sheep grazed had a pleasing appearance. When the rain stopped in the afternoon we rowed ashore. Some fishermen unloading their catch promptly gave us half a dozen haddock and one of them attached himself to us as guide. The post office was officially shut but our guide led us into the living room where the postmaster was dining *en famille* off some uncommonly strong fish soup. In spite of our protests he insisted on interrupting the meal to stamp our letters. Continuing our walk up the main street, ignoring a hardware shop and a clothes shop, we came to what looked like the third and last shop. Among a meagre window display we detected a ray of hope—a writing pad, an ink bottle, a packet of cigarettes, a few Westerns, and a bottle of beer. The stock inside was not much richer but we bought the beer bottle and had a suck all round, not forgetting our guide, for it was terribly expensive. The people of Midvaag, we decided, inclined to the literary life rather than the convivial. In the midst of this drinking bout it occurred to me that I had not yet entered the ship. There were no formalities at the Harbour-master's office beyond a cigar and a chat, and after he had rung up his confrère at the Customs house to tell him of our arrival, that concluded the ship's business. In the evening Charles and I followed the road out beyond the village and came eventually to a big lake, the Sorvaags Wand. The lake is peculiar in that it has no river emptying out but spills abruptly into the sea over a natural weir. The road, which leads to Sorvaag harbour on the west coast of Vaago, was built by British troops during the war, as was the airfield on Vaago, the only one in the Faeroes. From it there is a service to Glasgow and also to Iceland. The capital, Thorshavn, only two hours away by sea, is linked by a mail-boat. We were told that out of a total population of 36,000, 10,000 live in the capital; but this may be no more precise than another news item fed to the gullible visitors. We learnt that Midvaag's chief import is sheep's heads from Aberdeen, and considering the number of sheep to be seen grazing in the vicinity, all with heads, I found this hard to believe. Vaago like most of the other islands rises to over 2000 feet and the grazing is on the lower slopes near the sea. I doubt if anyone lives out of sight of the sea from which comes their food and their livelihood.

The Faeroe islander, therefore, is above all a seaman. In boats not much bigger than *Mischief* and less seaworthy, because they are powered only by an engine, they follow their calling across the Atlantic as well as round their windswept islands. The banks off the west coast of Greenland are well known to them. We had met Faeroe island boats at Godthaab. Crossing in May they spent the summer there, selling their catches to the local factories, and went home in the early autumn. Generally they had a crew of five, all housed in the fo'c'sle which was about the size of our galley. Their own galley was nothing more than a sort of wardrobe lashed on deck aft with a single gas ring inside. There was no question of working inside the galley, the cook merely opened the wardrobe door and stooped or knelt on deck to give the pot a stir.

From the Faeroes we had about 600 miles to go to Reykjavik which would be our port of departure for East Greenland. On the way there I had in mind a visit to the new volcanic island which had appeared off the south-west coast of Iceland on November 14th, 1963. To say the island 'appeared' is a mild description of its tumultuous birth, a birth attended by violent explosions which hurled clouds of smoke, steam, ash, and pumice thousands of feet into the air. By the next day, when wind blew away some of this cloud, it could be seen that an island had emerged from the sea. *Notices to Mariners* of January 23rd, 1964, contained the following warning: 'A submarine volcanic eruption has formed an island about half a mile in diameter and 250 feet high, in position 63° 18′ N. 20° 36′ W. Eruption is continuing and mariners are warned to keep clear of the area.' By April the island had grown to nearly a mile in length and 500 feet in height. It had been given the name Surtsey and the volcano itself was christened Surtur, after the Fire Giant Surtur of Norse mythology, who comes from the south when the world ends and burns up everything. In view of the overcast skies, the rain, and the fog that are common in those waters, I was not at all confident of being able to find this exciting island, let alone make a landing.

Before leaving Midvaag we stocked up with bread, fresh and warm from the bakery, neither so dark nor so heavy as the bread obtainable in Greenland. While I could stand any amount of it, one or two of the crew conceived for it such a dislike that they preferred to eat biscuit. By now Charles and I had repaired the huge tear in the genoa, a sail that we were able to hoist more often than I had looked for in those windy regions. Making over towards Iceland, generally under overcast skies, our navigation could not be as precise as one would wish when approaching that coast. 'The advisability of keeping at a distance cannot be too emphatically enjoined,' says the *Pilot*, 'and the numerous wrecks of British, German, French, Norwegian, Belgian, and Icelandic fishing vessels demonstrate strongly that the locality must be navigated with the utmost caution. For long stretches the coast is perfectly flat and from seaward it is difficult to make out the low coast against the high land of the interior, and it is frequently not seen until breakers are sighted. The land is bare of vegetation and the sand of which it is composed is, in many lights, indistinguishable from the sea.'

By the 24th June we were some fifty miles east of the Westman Islands or Vestmannaeyjar, Surtsey lying to the west of them. Of this group of islands twenty miles off the south coast of Iceland only Heimaey, the largest, is inhabited. The islands are remarkable for the wealth of bird life on their cliffs—puffins, fulmars, gannets—of which large numbers are taken by the islanders for food. Much now depended upon the weather. That afternoon we had a bit of a blow which soon subsided and the sunset looked promising. In northern latitudes, however, when the sun sets towards midnight and dawn follows soon after, a fine-weather sunset might equally be interpreted as the 'red sky in the morning when the sailor takes warning'. But June

25th proved to be our lucky day, bright, calm, and clear. At 6 a.m. we sighted the stacks and skerries of the westernmost islands and hard by them a great plume of cloud drifting away from a hump-backed island, its easy contours contrasting strangely with its wall-sided neighbours.

We spent the whole morning coming up with it and a large part of the afternoon poking about along its eastern shore for somewhere to anchor. To our surprise the shore shelved so steeply that close to the beach we found 4 fathoms of water and when we let go the anchor it merely slid off or through the ash into deeper water. As holding ground it was no better than a heap of flour. Finally we gave up and were content to let her drift while we launched the dinghy for Roger and I to go ashore. A small surf breaking on the beach did not hinder our landing though it did give a little trouble when we came to launch off.

The beach, of reddish-black sand or fine pumice, offered firm walking and even at that early period it had acquired some litter in the way of tins, bottles, and bits of wood. Beyond the narrow beach the ground sloped upwards to the summit at an angle of about 30°. On this ash slope it was like climbing a sandhill, two steps up and one down. I classed the climb, in Baedeker's words, as 'fatiguing and not rewarding', for the crater into which we finally peered belched merely smoke and fumes instead of the cauldron of molten, fiery lava that I had expected and hoped to see. There was a beacon on top, no doubt for survey purposes, so that evidently ours was not a first ascent except, no doubt, the first ascent by a British party. The whole place smelt like a coke oven. One sensed, too, that the thing was alive and growing but I must say I was staggered to see later in *The Times* of October 9th a picture of Surtsey and to learn that it had by then grown to 800 feet high.

The timing of our visit had been unlucky, or perhaps lucky, according to the point of view. I have since learnt that until April 4th 1964, Surtsey had been merely evidence of a marine eruption but on that date a lava eruption began when fountains of lava shot up to heights of 100 to 200 feet and numerous rivers of lava overflowed the crater to run into the sea. The greatest velocity in the lava flow was observed on April 22nd when a white-hot wave of lava covered a distance of 300 yards in fifteen seconds. The lava flow ceased at the end of April and for the next two and a half months no lava flowed over the crater rim, though it was probable that lava continued to flow into the sea from a vent below sea level. On July 9th lava began pouring out of the crater again, the level having by then become higher, and formed a lava lake about 100 yards in diameter. Thus at the time of our visit there was probably lava inside the crater but obscured from our view by smoke and steam. With the advent of lava, Surtsey's life is not likely to be as ephemeral as that of other volcanic islands. Of ten marine eruptions off Iceland in historic time, four built up islands and all four islands have been swallowed by the Atlantic. As long as Surtsey consisted only of volcanic ash and cinders its future was uncertain but since lava started to flow it is likely that the island will withstand the onslaught of the surf for a very long time despite the inroads that the surf has already made. In the winter of 1964, for example, a large chunk of the highest peak together with the survey beacon fell away, having been eroded at sea level.

The following account of Surtsey in action is from an article by Dr D. C. Blanchard, a scientist collecting data on the lightning and other electrical phenomena in the vicinity of the volcano:

> By this time Surtsey was three months old but the eruptions were still frequent. We approached from upwind and when we arrived Surtsey put on a magnificent display of the forces at her command. The eruptions were occurring from a crater near the edge of the island partially open to the sea. The contact of the cold sea water with the hot pumice or lava appeared to be the cause of giant explosions that sent geysers of ash-streaked cloud and water hurtling upwards to over a thousand feet. Cloud masses continued upwards until there was a long cloud column that extended from near the sea to heights of 20,000 feet. In the lowest thousand feet of the column there was frequent lightning and thunder; our instruments recorded the electrical activity. In addition we could see huge rocks or fire-bombs thrown out of the main plume to crash back on to the island or into the sea. Numerous mushroom-like clouds and smoke rings could be seen and from the lower parts of the plume a waterspout was visible against the dark curtain of ash that fell in long streamers to the sea.

With *Mischief* unattached to the bottom we did not want to linger long. When Roger had finished filming we collected some lava as souvenirs for the crew and then ran down in long, plunging strides as one might descend a slope of soft snow. We had been lucky with the weather. A day later there would have been no landing on Surtsey, a day of fierce and frequent squalls when we had to hand the jib and put four rolls in the mainsail. Having rounded Reykjanes, the south-western extremity of Iceland, we sailed briskly all night with a fine beam wind and early on June 27th anchored outside the dock entrance at Reykjavik. Our curry-powder 'Q,' flag attracted no attention so finally Bob Cook and I rowed ashore. Securing the dinghy, we climbed up a sea-wall and over some railings to land in a main thoroughfare where cars had stopped and a small crowd gathered to watch this English invasion. A man who spoke English at once offered to drive me to the harbour offices. There, with little ado, *Mischief* and her crew were entered and cleared at the same time at a cost of ten shillings, and the Harbour-master pointed out a fish wharf where we could lie.

Having motored in and made fast alongside a small fishing boat we were boarded by one of her crew, already more than a little drunk. Our gin was too mild for friend Gunnar who produced from his pocket a bottle of evil-tasting spirit known locally as 'Black Death', a name it richly deserved. It was a Saturday, after one o'clock and the shops closed, and we looked like being without either bread or beer over the week-end. Gunnar, his good nature inflamed and his wits unimpaired by 'Black Death', grasped the implications in a flash. He assured us we could forget the beer because in Reykjavik, or all Iceland for that matter, there was no such thing unless you counted the non-alcoholic beer brewed by permission of a government which knew what was good for you. As for bread, we should have that at once. Gunnar, Charles, and I, linking arms for mutual support, started for the town. Hailing the first available taxi Gunnar took us to a ship's chandlers where he battered pitilessly upon the door until it opened. As friends of his we received a moderately hearty welcome. There was, of course, no bread there but Gunnar, after receiving advice, went off again with Charles in the taxi, leaving the ship's chandler and I to drink each other's health in non-alcoholic beer. So we got our bread and presently managed to get rid of Gunnar. He would not hear of our paying off the taxi but continued in it alone, evidently feeling the need of fresh air and carriage exercise.

On Sunday we had a stream of visitors, some sober, some drunk. Charles and I who were on board alone almost had a fight with one who could not be persuaded to leave. In spite or because of the strict drinking rules the people of Reykjavik seemed of a convivial nature. Many of them are fishermen and sailors, traditionally free spenders, bent on making the most of their short spells on shore. The State brewery responsible for the revolting beer also makes spirits which are strictly rationed and which are in consequence readily obtainable 'under the counter'.

We thought Reykjavik an expensive place, particularly for eating. But we soon found a well-run Sailor's Institute where good, cheap meals were served cafeteria fashion, the helpings liberal, and a second helping to be got for nothing. At the same place there were hot showers. Most of the private houses, shops, and buildings are heated by natural hot water pumped from thermal springs at Reykir, ten miles distant. At Reykir, too, there are extensive greenhouses where things like tomatoes are grown. They even grow bananas there, though speaking as a banana-critic, one who has eaten them in most of their natural habitats and who once lived entirely on them for nine weeks in the course of a long cycle ride, I should regard Iceland bananas more as a curiosity than as edible fruit.

Reykjavik has 70,000 inhabitants out of a total Icelandic population of 170,000. In this respect it seems to be comparatively an even more powerful magnet than our own Great Wen. There are now too many corrugated iron and cement buildings, but the small Parliament House of stone, set in a neat little square, is solid and dignified. The most attractive feature to me is the way the town surrounds and is a part of the harbour and docks, a street having on one side houses and on the other ships. Fish and fishing are its business. Where we lay the small inshore fishing boats were in and out almost every day, lorries awaiting to take the fish to the nearby processing factory, one of several. We had to pass this on our way to town and were frequently given half a dozen fish from the heap that a lorry had just dumped on the floor. Naturally in our neighbourhood the smell of fish was all pervading. 'He who would have eggs must bear with cackling.'

Prince Philip was about to visit Reykjavik in the royal yacht and a number of British journalists were gathering there. Two, representing a popular daily, had arrived prematurely and while kicking their heels waiting tried to make some 'copy' out of *Mischief*. It had been expected that if the royal yacht met a British trawler off Iceland the Duke of Edinburgh would probably board her, and these two journalists, taking a sporting chance, had taken passage on a trawler from Hull. Unluckily, while hanging about south of Iceland in the hope of meeting Britannia the trawler had caught no fish. The skipper, soon tiring of this, sailed for north Iceland and landed his two passengers. They came to see us one evening, taking the needless precaution of bringing their own whisky. They were good company, the night wore on, until at around midnight they decided that their paper would like some pictures of *Mischief* and her crew. It seemed to me a little dark for successful photographs. Maybe they had some confused notions of being in the Land of the Midnight Sun. However, we obliged them by draping ourselves round the shrouds in picturesque attitudes and with difficulty dissuaded the photographer from climbing the mast.

On June 30th most of the ships in the harbour dressed overall in honour of *Britannia*'s expected arrival. As we were the only British representative we took it upon ourselves to sail out into the roads to pay our respects. In the afternoon, with our big Blue Ensign flying from the peak of the gaff we sailed out of the harbour into the buoyed channel. Fortunately we had time in hand because in making a trial salute the halyard parted and we had to lower the mainsail in order to reeve another. Except for an Icelandic gunboat we were the only vessel waiting outside. At 4 p.m., exactly on time, *Britannia* and her escort H.M.S. *Malcolm* hove in sight, and, the wind being fair, we sailed past her on a reciprocal course about a cable's length away. Grand she looked with her shining dark blue hull and three slender masts flying the Icelandic flag, the Royal Standard, and the Duke of Edinburgh's own standard, and at her stern the largest White Ensign I have ever seen. It was a proud moment for *Mischief* and her crew when this huge ensign was dipped to acknowledge our salute and when the Duke stepped out of the chart-room to give us a friendly wave. We were back in time to witness the official reception when he landed at the harbour steps.

Before leaving Iceland a few days later the Duke held a reception for all British residents in Reykjavik at the British Ambassador's residence. I scarcely qualified, but having known the Ambassador some years before in Rangoon I, too, was invited. There must have been at least a hundred people present and it was most impressive to see how the Duke conversed in turn with everyone there and often managed to joke with them. On a less exalted plane we met one or two interesting people. There was the Reykjavik golf professional, a Welshman. Iceland and golf seem somehow incongruous, though no more so, I suppose, than golf in the Magellan Straits where it is played at Punta Arenas on what surely must be the windiest course in the world. Then there was the Iceland Airways pilot who came to have a look at *Mischief*—a native Icelander, and in 1940 barely out of school, he had gone to England to join the R.A.F. as a fighter pilot, a quite remarkable case, I thought, of enterprise and courage. We found a good friend, too, in the captain of a Danish cargo vessel who dispensed Carlsberg lager with the utmost generosity. He had with him a handsome Alsatian dog which he oddly named Henry Morgan. Like beer, dogs are prohibited in Reykjavik, but the police were wise enough to look the other way when Henry Morgan took a walk on the quay.

Charles Marriott, who has a tourist's mind, contemplated an excursion. He could not bear to leave Iceland without seeing a geyser and a waterfall. Enquiries showed that Great Geyser and Gullfoss waterfall could be reached by bus and that there was a hotel nearby. Even when on pleasure bent, Charles, like Mrs Gilpin, has a frugal mind; so he took a rucksack and a one-man tent, determined to sleep outside and eat inside. Geysers have generally to be encouraged before they will perform. One approaches them, as it were, according to the Pathan proverb, 'a lump of gur* in one hand and a stone in the other' though in the case of geysers it is soap or sods. In *Letters from High Latitudes* we read how Lord Dufferin's party spent three days waiting for Great Geyser and were rewarded only after a sharp emetic in the form of a cart-load of sods had been administered. Since his time quantities of soap have been found more effective. Charles spent a wet night in his tent and from his subdued account we gathered that neither he nor the other tourists present at Great Geyser were sufficiently provided with soap or sods. Roger Coward, who wanted film material,

---

*   Gur—jaggery or unrefined sugar.

persuaded the rest of the crew to club together to charter a motor car for their sight-seeing tour.

The only ice information obtainable concerned Icelandic waters where the pack-ice was reported unusually close to the north coast—within twenty miles in fact. I therefore visited H.M.S. *Malcolm* where they listened to and interpreted for me the ice report broadcast daily from Angmagssalik. It indicated the presence of heavy polar ice extending fifteen miles out from Angmagssalik and the adjoining coast. This was certainly discouraging. At Skjoldungen 100 miles further south conditions might be better, and during the week or more that it would take us to cross Denmark Strait things might improve. It was still early in the season and should the ice on inspection prove to be unnavigable we could always go round Cape Farewell to the west coast, either to find some mountains to climb or to wait. On July 6th when we had intended to sail it was blowing hard. On the advice of the fishermen, reinforced by a weather report from H.M.S. *Exmouth* who had just arrived, we postponed our departure for a day.

CHAPTER XI

ANGMAGSSALIK

———◆———

THE CAUTIOUS DELAYING of our start did not save us from running into some rough weather. *Mischief* is so good a seaboat that down below amidships the motion is seldom violent, yet on this occasion our teapot—a heavy, squat, six-pint affair—leapt right off the table. After so long a spell ashore poor Noddy was seasick and I lost overboard what I called my Hudson Bay hat, a hideous thing such as is worn by baseball players, given to me gratis at the Hudson Bay Company store at Pond Inlet because none of their Eskimo customers would look at it. We had knocked off 100 miles before this blow subsided and left us becalmed. We did some repairs to the sails and four of us had a very brief swim over the side. Has anyone before bathed voluntarily in Denmark Strait? The sea temperature was still 50°, for the Irminger current, a branch of the comparatively warm Atlantic current, impinges against the south coast of Iceland before flowing west across Denmark Strait to merge finally with the cold East Greenland current.

A halo round the sun and a falling glass heralded another blow which overtook us that night when we had to heave to, the wind being contrary. After this the wind settled in northeast and remained fair and light for the rest of the passage. We sighted a small Danish cargo vessel bound west; she had the characteristic red hull of most of the vessels seen in Greenland waters. We tried to speak her but she went on her way. On July 12th, in spite of some fog, I managed to get sights which put us some twenty miles east of Cape Dan. At this point the coast changes direction from south-west to west, forming a sort of bight at the back of which lies Angmagssalik about fifteen miles west and a little south of the cape. Off the cape the currents are strong and much ice frequently accumulates. It surprised us that so far we had seen neither bergs nor pack-ice for we were well in the East Greenland current. Both sea and air temperatures had dropped to 40°. In these waters, too, the presence of fog, such as we were then meeting, often indicates the presence of ice.

On account of more fog that evening we set a double watch and at 1 a.m., in very murky conditions, we passed a big berg and some scattered floes. We sailed slowly on under staysail alone steering west until at 6 a.m. of the 13th we became entangled among thick floes. Starting the engine we retreated south-east into open water. In spite of fog we could distinguish the ice edge, so we began sailing south well outside it hoping that in the latitude of Skjoldungen there might be less ice. Obviously the ice off Angmagssalik was too heavy for us to navigate. Whether or not we reached Angmagssalik did not much matter. Politeness required that if possible we should report our presence on the coast and we were naturally curious to see what the only town in East Greenland looked like.

There now occurred another of those chance meetings that so often decide the course of events for good or for ill. In this case the chance meeting, though it resulted in our reaching Angmagssalik, brought about nothing but ill. In the course of the morning we sighted a cargo vessel of about 4000 tons, stationary. By midday we were within speaking distance of each other and having a good 'gam'. Like the royal yacht she was named *Britannia*. Bound for Angmagssalik from the West Greenland coast she had been waiting there six days for ice conditions to improve. Her captain added that a local vessel was on her way out to lead him through the ice and he appeared to assume that we would take advantage of this opportunity. *Ejnar Mikkelsen* presently arrived. She was small, possibly about 200 tons, a Norwegian sealer-type specially built for manoeuvring in ice, with 240 h.p. engines, enormously thick hull, and rounded bows—a sort of miniature ice-breaker. Without the debate and deliberation that such a dubious step required it was taken for granted that we should follow in the wake of these two vessels. I suppose I ought to have known better, but I confess I did not anticipate our having much difficulty in following behind them. So, in happy ignorance of what was in store, we now devoted ourselves to getting into trouble with complete success.

The convoy got under way and for the first half-hour, the ice cover being 5/10 or less, we managed pretty well. Even so we failed to keep close under *Britannia*'s stern as we had been adjured to do. Going at

Ejnar Mikkelsen returning to open a lead

our best speed of five or six knots in order to keep up, with ice all around we were bound to hit some, and this we could not afford to do however small the ice might be. When the floes thickened to 7/10 or more they had to slacken speed while *Ejnar Mikkelsen* opened a way through, thus allowing us to come up close astern of *Britannia*. We were not there long. As soon as she forged ahead the wash from her propeller made *Mischief* unsteerable. Her head was thrown off to one side and sometimes we found ourselves facing the wrong way. Nor could we prevent ourselves from falling further and further behind. The floes that closed in *Britannia*'s wake slowed us down or stopped us altogether, so that eventually we would become completely boxed in by ice, unable to move in any direction, and the two ships ahead almost lost to sight in the fog. Twice *Ejnar Mikkelsen* had to come back to open a lead for us or even to throw us a rope in order to haul our bows round. With her small propeller on the port quarter *Mischief* is about as manoeuvrable as a steam-roller and quite impossible to turn round in a confined space.

At 4 p.m. when we had done about two miles and were again completely stuck we noticed that the two ships ahead had also stopped and were apparently conferring together. We stepped on to the ice to take photographs of *Mischief* in trouble as well as to warm ourselves. It was bitterly cold in the damp fog, the temperature just above freezing point. *Ejnar Mikkelsen* then started back towards us, shouldering aside massive floes as big or bigger than herself or smashing them under her bows. She stopped nearby, her Greenlander crew grinning cheerfully, very much at home in these dismal, frigid surroundings, her two or three passengers huddled up in coats and mufflers regarding us, we thought, with sour looks. Her skipper joined us on the ice. Niels Underborg, who now and later proved a good friend to us, thick-set, ruddy complexioned, bare-headed, looked a proper seaman. He and *Britannia*'s captain had been discussing what was best to do, whether to push on or whether to take us back to open water; they had agreed that *Britannia* should make her own way and that *Ejnar Mikkelsen* should look after us. We expressed regret at making a nuisance of ourselves but he did not seem to mind and fully appreciated our difficulties, especially in keeping close astern. On the other hand, the two or three passengers he had on board seemed to mind quite a lot.

A Danish girl, smoking a pipe, had been particularly vociferous and vehement in word and gesture, urging us to go faster. More important than this pipe-smoking Amazon was the Governor of Angmagssalik District who was also on board, and who, impatient at the delay, wanted Niels to abandon us. He, of course, would not hear of this, knowing that we had no chance at all of getting out of the ice without assistance. He said we had still about twelve miles of ice to negotiate and again urged us to keep close, for owing to the strong currents no lead remained open for long.

We started once more, the ice as thick as ever, the fog worse, no hint anywhere of land. There is a radio beacon on Cape Dan so presumably Niels was using that and the Angmagssalik radio station to maintain direction. Again we became hemmed in by ice and had to be extricated and several times we just scraped through between moving floes at a cost of nothing but loss of paint. Many of the floes had long under-water projections, easily discernible by the light green colour above them, though it was difficult to guess what depth of water covered them. One of these projecting tongues now proved both our undoing and our salvation. When trying to squeeze through a gap between two floes our keel grounded on the projecting tongue of one. Unable to move we stuck there while the floe to port, topping our deck by a good six feet inexorably closed. Poor *Mischief* gave a shudder as she was lifted up, canted over, and the port-side bulwarks crushed in with the frightening noise of rending timber. I had just begun to think of what we most needed to take if we had to pile out on the ice in a hurry, when the floes drifted slowly apart and *Mischief* slid off the ice. Apparently the projecting tongue had hit the opposing floe and had rebounded. Our relief was premature. Noddy, who was below at the engine controls while I steered and shouted orders down to him, reported the well full and water overflowing into the cabin. Manning the barrel pump on deck we soon had the leak under control. But we could not let-up. She was leaking freely and the pump had to be kept going. It was now about midnight, still foggy, and still no sign of land. But the ice showed signs of relenting. We began to find long leads of more or less open water in which we could do our five knots and in these easier conditions I handed over the tiller where I had been for the last twelve hours. At last at 4 a.m. some high land showed close at

Sailing in Angmagssalik Fjord

hand above the fog, and shortly after we sensed rather than saw that we were within a fjord entrance. The floes were thicker in the fjord and the fog worse. We lost sight of *Ejnar Mikkelsen* and stopped, for we had no idea where the harbour lay. She soon came back, we half heard some shouted instructions about avoiding a wire, and then we followed into the harbour where she anchored. We made fast alongside her, thankful to have arrived, albeit in so leaky a condition. It was a bit early for breakfast but not too early for a drink. Niels Underborg, before retiring to his house on shore, joined us. He spoke excellent English having served for three years during the war with the Worcestershire Regiment. He thought that we were lucky to be in and that it might be three weeks before we should be able to get out.

Leaving the pump manned the rest of us turned in for some sleep. When we came on deck again we might have been in a different world. Instead of the cold, Stygian gloom in which we had been enveloped for so long, we beheld the fairest of sunlit scenes. From a cloudless, azure sky the sun shone benignly, flooding with warm light the rock ridges and snow couloirs of the mountains across the fjord. The ice floes dotting the fjord, which yesterday had been dull, grey menacing shapes, now sparkled joyously on the crystal blue water. The 100-yard-wide harbour entrance was bounded on one side by an unoccupied wharf and on the other by a wall of rock. Between, supported on buoys, lay a wire which served more or less effectively to stop floes from drifting into the harbour. The small harbour shallowed quickly to where a fast-running river with a bridge over it flowed in. At this shallow end were landing steps and a wharf for small craft with two big warehouses on it. Behind, clustered on the steep hillside, lay the brightly coloured buildings of the town.

Niels had advised us that at the shallow end there was a bit of beach where we could lay *Mischief* on her side, and that a Danish shipwright carpenter, Martin, would be able to patch her up. Meantime we had to keep the pump going and on that account maintained the usual two-hour watches. A few strokes of the pump every minute or so sufficed to keep the water in check. I went ashore to have a look at the hard where we were to beach *Mischief* and to make arrangements with Martin. He, too, had some English and told us that we could beach the boat that evening at high water and that at midnight the water would be low enough for him to start work. At that time of year it was light all night and Martin was willing to work at any hour.

We were a little uneasy about laying *Mischief* over with all the stores and ballast inside. If the bottom were uneven or if she lay down on a bit of rock, we might do her more harm than good. However, we could see the bottom clearly and at the top of the tide we got her in a good position, put plenty of weight on the starboard side, and as the water fell she lay down quietly enough until she came to rest on the turn of the bilge at an angle of about 50°. On the port side we could see two separate damaged places where several planks had been sprung. At midnight Martin turned up and he had time to cut out some of the damaged planks and insert short lengths of new wood before the water returned. As the water rose and began lapping over the starboard deck *Mischief* lay inert, seemingly content to end a life of toil on the beach at Angmagssalik. We suffered a few minutes of extreme alarm. The trouble was that she had a lot of water inside. When the tide went down and she began to list over the pump had no longer sucked; all this water was now swishing about in the cabin up to the top of my bunk. Moreover, as she began to list to starboard, we had forgotten to haul back the boom which we had swung out to weight her on that side, and once she was on her side it was impossible to shift it. Needless to say she came upright long before the water had risen enough to lap over the cockpit coaming, but not before I had become grey with anxiety.

We remained where we were until at 1 p.m. next day, when she was again on the beach, Martin completed the repairs on that side. Before putting her down again starboard side uppermost in order to have a look at that side we went back to a buoy to get some sleep, having had only about three hours in the last two days. It was impossible to eat or sleep on board while she was lying over. We ate on the beach surrounded by urchins, huskies, oil, and harbour offal, and slept where we could. Charles took his tent and camped by the river. She still leaked, though nothing like so badly. When we came to look at the starboard side we found the wood badly scarred forward of midships. Martin probed this carefully and apparently satisfied himself that none of the planks had been cracked right through. He did some caulking there and also round the rudder trunk.

On the beach at Angmagssalik undergoing repairs

By now *Britannia* had come safely in and was unloading at the quay. Her captain proved most friendly, bore us no grudge for the delay we had caused him, and seemed more concerned at our misadventures. In between high and low water, when we were either putting *Mischief* on the hard or floating her off, we explored Angmagssalik. Beer could be bought at the Greenland Trading Company store, but not drunk there, and there was a small coffee bar. Down by the river we found a communal wash-house where for ten ore one could have a hot shower and the use of a washing machine. There were usually a number of Greenlander women gossiping there and since they were more familiar with washing machines they seldom allowed us to wash our own clothes. For the fourth time we careened *Mischief*, as she was still making a lot of water. This time we put her on stern first in order to have the stern well clear of the water for inspection. Martin could find nothing there. We turned her round and went on again bow first. At 4 a.m. Martin came to put a sheet of lead, felt, and finally a sheet of zinc, covering the whole of the damaged area on the port side. This appeared to do the trick.

We had hoped to get away that day. As yet there was no chance of our going out to sea and south to Skjoldungen, but we could at least cross King Oscar's Havn, as the local fjord was named, to climb a mountain there; or we might possibly go up the much larger Angmagssalik Fjord between Cape Dan and the mainland which runs north for nearly thirty miles. By keeping close inshore we could avoid the heavy ice which still blocked our escape to sea. And not only our escape. *Britannia* had already made an attempt to sail and had had to return. But the brilliant weather we had enjoyed now broke; a gale of wind ushered in four days of incessant rain. Nor was this the only 'trifling sum of misery added to the foot of our account'. Too late we discovered that between Friday and Monday no beer was to be had; a local bye-law to that effect ensured that on pay-day the Greenlander would have to take some of his money home. Niels Underborg asked us to his house where he showed us a number of charming pictures of Greenland scenes which he had painted. He told us of the fate of *Ejnar Mikkelsen*'s predecessor which had been capsized by an ice floe off Cape Dan and had sunk in less than five minutes. He and the crew had all managed to get on to the ice whence they were soon picked up.

Anchored outside Angmagssalik Harbour

Ejnar Mikkelsen, by the way, is the name of a noted Danish explorer
and administrator of East Greenland who, although now eighty years
old, still visits the country. We were entertained, too, by our pipe-
smoking girl friend to coffee and delicious cakes. She proved not to be
the Amazon I had feared but a charming, friendly schoolmistress who
taught in the local school and who thoroughly enjoyed life at Angmagssalik. Her gestures during our adventures in the ice had evidently
been of encouragement rather than of impatience.

Although on the Tuesday, July 21st, rain still fell we made an
attempt to reach Angmagssalik Fjord. By ten o'clock we were back
at the buoy having found the ice too thick and *Mischief* too unhandy.
From our first day here a peak on the far side of King Oscar's Havn
had roused our interest, a peak named on the chart Poljemsfjeld,
or in Eskimo Qimertajalik, of graceful shape, with two steep ridges
enclosing a long snow couloir. So a day later, having collected some
white bread kindly baked for us by the wife of the harbour master we
motored across to an anchorage within striking distance of our mountain. It is only 3380 feet high so that even I could expect to get up and
down in the day. Bob Cook, Charles Sewell, and I left the boat at 10.30
and an hour later had reached the foot of the peak. Two hours scram-
bling over easy rocks brought us to the bottom of the snow couloir. In
spite of the late hour the snow remained in prime condition for kicking
steps. For the next hour we climbed in this glistening couloir, encouraged by the knowledge that it would bring us out close to the summit.
By 2.30 p.m. we were on top, happy in our success and in the magnificent prospect extending over miles of ice-covered sea to the blue water
beyond. In a small cairn we found a tin with records of two earlier
ascents—the first in 1931 by two Germans, and the second in 1954 by
two Danes.

By the time we started down the sun had softened the snow in the
couloir. We roped up with Charles in front and Bob, the heavyweight,
in rear as anchorman. Care was needed, for our upgoing steps were apt
to give way and underneath the snow lay ice. At a point about halfway
down Bob was not quite careful enough. The step broke and down he
shot knocking me off my steps and finally pulling off Charles. Fortunately the couloir made a sharp bend just below and before we had
fallen fifty feet the three of us fetched up on the rocks in a tangle of

rope and ice-axes with no hurt except to our self-esteem. On our way back to the boat we took what we hoped would be a shorter route. Whichever way you go, the Spanish proverb tells us, there is a league of bad road. Having made long detours to avoid cliffs and crossed innumerable gullies, we reached the boat at 7 p.m. in about twice as long a time as that of the outward journey.

CHAPTER XII

HOMEWARD BOUND

O N RETURNING TO THE HARBOUR we saw a very stoutly built, wooden, Norwegian trading vessel. *Ardvark* had just returned from Skjoldungen where there is a small settlement and her captain told us he had met a lot of ice and strongly advised us not to try yet awhile. On the 25th, therefore, we made a short excursion into Angmagssalik Fjord. Dodging among ice floes until evening we finally anchored in a branch fjord called Sangmalik. We noticed that although we were only some fifteen miles from Angmagssalik heavy banks of snow lay all along the beach while a lake, only a few feet above sea level, was covered with ice two to three feet thick. Nothing whatever grew there, whereas at Angmagssalik grass and flowers abound. I attributed this to the fact that Sangmalik, on the opposite side of the peninsula on which Poljemsfjeld lies, faces north.

Bob and I had a day's climbing on Sofiasfjeld, much the same height as our first peak, treading snow all the way except for a bit of loose rock on the summit ridge. We could look inland to the ice cap and seaward to Cape Dan where the ice appeared as thick as ever. The glacier by which we descended had its foot in the lake, a fact which would certainly encourage the lake to remain frozen. On the return passage we took advantage of a breeze to launch the dinghy and take pictures of *Mischief* under sail. Beating down the main fjord against the wind we met in turn *Ejnar Mikkelsen* and *Ardvark* bound up the fjord to the settlement of Kungmiut. We were a little dismayed to find that this short spell of beating in sheltered water sufficed to reopen the leak.

Martin came on board and although we pulled up floor boards and emptied lockers we failed to track it down. He had brought with him a bag of sawdust. Securing the boathook to the handle of a bucket filled with sawdust he plunged the bucket down beneath the hull and at the same time contrived to spill out the sawdust. In theory the sawdust is sucked into the leak by the ingoing water and bungs it up.

Provided one knows whereabouts on the hull to spill the bucket this trick works; and it worked then although the leak had not been located and was not very pronounced. With that we should have to be content. Having already beached her five times we were not likely to discover anything fresh by doing it once more.

After nearly a fortnight we were becoming impatient to go. As Dr Johnson observed: 'Patience is a virtue very easily fatigued by exercise.' We filled up with oil and water, made our farewells to the harbour master, Martin, and other well-wishers, and on July 31st sailed out to try conclusions with the ice. By 4 p.m. we slunk back. Two miles out we had met with heavy ice and from the masthead had seen nothing but ice. For the sake of exercise most of us at various times had walked up the hill behind the town known locally as Seaman's Hill. I preferred to call it 'Spy-glass Hill'. Close on 2000 feet high, it afforded an excellent view seawards. When I went up there before breakfast next day I saw what I took to be a possible lead through the ice. We motored out at 9 a.m. steering for some icebergs I had noted as leading marks. From deck-level the lead looked a lot less open and owing to a heavy swell the floes were rising and falling in a frightening way. After getting ourselves nearly shut in, and taking ten minutes to turn the boat round, we scuttled back to harbour in a chastened mood.

Early next morning I was again up Spy-glass, this time climbing to the higher southernmost summit, known as Somansfjeldet (2400 feet) whence one could see south along the coast. What I saw inspired me with fresh hope. We started after breakfast, hugging the coast until we came to an unmistakable berg which I had marked down as the point for us to turn seawards. Motoring up a wide lead with only a few scattered floes we congratulated ourselves on having won clear. But at midday we ran into pretty solid ice and from the masthead no open water could be seen. Back we had to go. I climbed Spy-glass Hill for the third morning running less in the hope of seeing a fresh lead than with the need to convince myself that we had really met ice the previous day and had not imagined it. This useful exercise showed me convincingly how quickly ice conditions could change. Where we had been motoring in open water was now all ice.

In order to leave more room in the cramped harbour we moved outside to a small bay where we were sometimes woken by being nudged by stray floes. On one occasion we found ourselves sitting, as it were, on an ice saddle, our keel over the sunken middle section of a floe with the two above-water parts of it on either side. On yet another pilgrimage up Spy-glass Hill on the evening of August 4th I met a solitary Dane coming down. We had a brief and baffling chat from which I concluded that either his English or mine must be faulty. 'Have you been to the top?' I asked. 'I live there,' came the reply. 'Oh! What do you do there?' 'I cook!'

The ice still looked unpromising but Niels, who came on board that night, spoke encouragingly and told us that on the way back from Cape Dan he had seen from his wheelhouse for the first time that summer the open sea. I spent the next two days in bed with a chill but when our look-out returned from Spy-glass on the evening of the 6th he reported the bay more or less ice-free. We stupidly deferred sailing till next morning when Roger, who had gone up the hill early to confirm this, reported ice all across the fjord entrance. Early on the 8th the report was the same, but that afternoon, which was marvellously fine and clear, several of us climbed Spy-glass for what was to be the last time. Nowhere could we see any ice thick enough to stop us. Our chance had come.

We sailed on August 9th and by midday had reached the open sea. Until we were clear of the ice it was bitterly cold. We hoisted sail and drifted southwards with the current, the sea perfectly calm, the afternoon warm and sunny. Throughout the next day in light airs we progressed slowly, noting with some misgiving the bergs and pack-ice all along between us and the shore. We knew, however, that the appearance of pack-ice from a distance is often deceptive and we felt that when the time came to go in the ice would be navigable. We were to have no chance of testing this.

On the 11th in fog and a fresh south-east wind we began at last to move smartly. The wind presently backed north-west and freshened to Force 5 as the fog cleared. Closing the land we identified Cape Mosting, about thirty miles from Skjoldungen, and were then forced further out to sea by a projecting cape of ice. That was as near as we were to get to our objective. Under the strains of fast sailing the leak had started again and every two hours at the change of watch about 500 strokes of the pump were needed to clear the well. By 7 p.m. this had increased to 900 strokes and after a brief talk with the crew, who were naturally disappointed, I decided to head for home. I felt that with the menace of this leak hanging over us we should not much enjoy the short time we had left for Skjoldungen. Nor could we mend matters by returning to Angmagssalik to put the boat once again on the beach. We could steer a northerly course towards Iceland and the Faeroes, so that if the leak worsened, as I feared it might, we should have a chance to put in.

So in the gathering gloom of a wild night of wind and rain we turned her head eastwards. We wanted to steer north-east but it was by now blowing hard and we did not want to make the leak worse by sailing close on the wind. As it was the pump had to be kept going more or less continuously. We doubled the watch, one man steering while the other stood by in the cockpit to pump vigorously every few minutes until the pump sucked dry. Rain continued throughout the next day and when we found ourselves unable to steer better than south-west, we hove to. This lessened the leak considerably and we derived much comfort from the knowledge that at the cost of standing still we could at any rate keep afloat.

Two days of wet, gloomy weather, accompanied by northerly winds that prevented us steering a northerly course, did little to cheer us. We found that she leaked most when on the port tack and that in light winds one man could cope with both steering and pumping. During a calm spell we launched the dinghy to see if we could repeat Martin's successful trick with sawdust, having brought a bag of it with us. There was too much of a lop. Apart from covering the surface of the water with sawdust we achieved nothing. We even tried hauling an old sail under the hull, a remedy that obviously could be effective only if there was a large hole with water pouring in. Another search inside the hull led nowhere. The number of damp patches and weeps we discovered did not account for the steady trickle into the well. I suppose we became accustomed to living in a leaking ship just as in time one becomes accustomed to living with noise, pain, and the other ills of life. As the sage observed: 'Human life is everywhere a state where much is to be endured and little enjoyed.' We forgot about Iceland, still as far off as ever, and decided to steer direct for the Western islands and the North Channel.

Homeward bound across the Atlantic one expects and seldom gets a steady stream of westerly winds. A fine northerly breeze lasted for a day and a half giving us a good push to the southeast, and with brighter weather we were able to get sights. At various times two large schools of porpoises chased us for hours leaping clear into the air and turning somersaults. 'When the sea-hog jumps', they say 'stand to your pumps.' On this occasion, as on others, the adage proved false and in any case our pump was already manned. The wind died at night and even a crimson sunrise provoked nothing but light winds for the next two days.

It was not until the 20th that we began really to move as the wind increased slowly to gale force until by the next day we were running at three knots under bare poles. As often happens we neglected to rig the canvas cover over the skylight before those below had suffered some salt water showers. The deck pump which had seen some pretty hard usage in the last few weeks chose this moment to break, the wooden plunger coming adrift from the actuating rod. The spare rotary pump fitted in the heads was awkward to use and called for a lot of effort. Nobody much cared for it. So Charles Marriott and Noddy, representing respectively advanced scientific theory and applied mechanics, got to work, and with screw-hooks and wire contrived a lash-up for the barrel pump. It worked provided it was gently used.

On a warm, windless day after the gale the *Ocean Ranger* of Manchester passed close by. When we called her by lamp asking to be reported she merely responded with three blasts on her siren. At dawn of the 27th I got a fix with star sights and in consequence altered course in order to have a good look at Rockall, the lone rock out in the Atlantic 200 miles west of St Kilda. Having come up with it we sailed round half a cable away from this remarkable rock upon which very few landings have been made. The sea being perfectly calm I had entertained hopes of landing, but as we drew near we could see that even the slight swell then running broke in violence as it hit the rock. Rockall is 70 feet high and about 80 feet on the water-line, steep all round and the east face quite sheer. Nothing like granite. For ages this diminutive rock has faced the fierce Atlantic gales and there it still stands defiant and apparently little diminished.

On the evening of August 29th we sighted the Dubh Artach light off Iona and for good measure the loom of Skerryvore, Inishtrahull, and Islay lights. I for one was not sorry to know that at last we had some land within reach. With a favouring tide we whistled through Rathlin Sound and had arrived off our old acquaintance Red Bay just as it turned against us. On three occasions we have had to anchor there to avoid a foul tide but this time with a light northerly wind we could just stem the tide.

At Barmouth, where I live, *Mischief* was known only by name. I had promised to bring her there one day and now was the chance. At least we could have the barrel pump properly repaired; and although I wanted to be back earlier than usual, having engaged to fly to Australia on October 20th to sail a vessel to Heard Island in the Southern Ocean, we still had time in hand. Accordingly, instead of heading for Land's End we altered course to pass south of the Isle of Man and thence to Holyhead, the nearest port to Barmouth at which we could get Customs clearance.

We had run into an anticyclone with fine, hazy weather and easterly winds, blowing, as winds so often do, from precisely the place for which one is bound. The haze became fog which persisted off and on for the next week. We spent an unpleasant night off the Isle of Man with not a glimmer of the Chicken Rock light and ships hooting anxiously all round us. As we beat towards Anglesey on September 1st against a hard southeast wind we were only dimly aware of our position. However, we sighted the Skerries late that evening and at 2 a.m. anchored outside the Holyhead breakwater. At daylight we entered the New Harbour and anchored near the coastguard station attracted there by the sight of a man cleaning the windows. Rowing ashore I explained that we were bound for Barmouth and asked him to rouse out a Customs officer to clear us. He knew the Barmouth coastguard, Mr R. H. Williams, commonly known as Bob Henry, a Barmouth worthy, town councillor and monumental mason, a sociable man who, if need be, could outsing a choir of convivial canaries. He promised to telephone Bob Henry and I was not quick enough to stop him, for I feared the consequences.

At eight o'clock a Customs officer came off and cleared us with a minimum of fuss and an hour later we sailed. We were just in time. Shortly after, as we heard on the wireless, fog prevented any ships entering or leaving Holyhead. It was about sixty miles to Barmouth

Icebergs

Rockall

and had we motored all the way, as we had no intention of doing, we could not have arrived before 9 p.m., too late to cross the bar. As it was we took our time. Having drifted past the South Stack we were accosted by a launch and told pretty shortly to clear out five miles to seaward as we were in a guided missile range. The day, though hazy, was altogether too lovely to be marred by motoring. We pointed to our idle sails, asked them to send us a wind, and left it at that. Throughout the afternoon, in happy ignorance of what was then passing at Barmouth, we sailed and drifted slowly on, passed through Bardsey Sound at 10 p.m., and at midnight sighted the Causeway buoy.

This buoy marks the western end of Sarn Badrig, or St Patrick's Causeway, which reaches out twelve miles into Cardigan Bay from a few miles north of Barmouth. At low water springs parts of it dry out and in the brief but glorious days of the Welsh schooners trading out of Portmadoc, Barmouth and Aberdovey, several vessels were wrecked there. This natural causeway runs so straight that it is easy to believe it to be man-made, one of the embankments of the legendary kingdom of Cantref-y-Gwaleod, the 'lowland hundred', now sunk beneath the waters of Cardigan Bay. Those who have read Peacock's *Misfortunes of Elphin* will remember the immortal drunkard Seithenyn, watchman of the embankment and answerable to the king for its safety, whose neglect allowed it to decay. During the great storm that finally engulfed the kingdom, breaching the neglected embankment and sweeping away all that were on it, Seithenyn, instead of being drowned like the rest as he deserved, got safely ashore on one of the hundreds of wine barrels to which he had devoted his life industriously emptying.

The entrance to Barmouth harbour is buoyed but not lit. Having run our distance from the Causeway buoy we took soundings and anchored in four fathoms at 5 a.m. I assumed we were off Barmouth but a wrong course had evidently been given to the helmsman or steered by mistake. When daylight came the familiar landmarks showed me that we were four miles to the south. Off we went motoring at speed in order to cross the bar on the flood tide. Going up the channel towards the harbour we were met by a local lobster boat: on board, the unquenchable Bob Henry with a television camera team. As we made towards the little stone quay, where flags and welcoming banners were still hanging, we realised what we had escaped, and what disappointment we had caused the previous afternoon, by failing to perform the impossible. Owing to miscalculations of distance, time, and *Mischief*'s abilities, a great part of Barmouth, led by the mayor, had awaited our arrival from three o'clock until dusk, telescopes sweeping the horizon and boats ranging the sea in search of us, at the time when we were still the wrong side of Bardsey Island.

Having made sure that *Mischief* would not fall over, for the quay dries out, I went home for breakfast. By the time I got back the flow of visitors had begun and throughout the day we were either show- ing people round the boat or were ourselves being stared at from the crowded quay. With *Mischief* high and dry no pumping was required and all hands proceeded in relays to Bodowen for baths and food.

Having had the pump repaired and spent a wet night at the *Last Inn* we sailed early on September 4th. An easterly breeze took us as far as the Sarn-y-Bwch buoy off Aberdovey where we were becalmed in fog. All night and next morning fog persisted until a south-west- erly breeze sprang up accompanied by rain. Visibility was not much improved but we identified Cardigan Island and that night picked up the loom of the Strumbles light. Passing well outside the South Bishop and Smalls we crossed the Bristol Channel with a fresh breeze at north- west and a rough sea. Next morning dawned thick and drizzly, the wind having backed south-west. It was no sort of weather in which to be approaching Land's End. We had neither seen nor heard anything since passing the Smalls and were pointing, so we thought, for the Scil- lies. The Bristol Channel and the adjacent coasts of Devon and Corn- wall are the scenes of *Mischief*'s youth but I can't understand why she chose at this time to take us into St Ives Bay. Steering a little west of south and seeing through a brief clearing in the murk some pleasantly green scenery on our starboard hand, I naturally took it for the Scil- lies. How fallible are human assumptions! Charles Marriott, who lives in these wild regions, tentatively suggested it might be St Ives, and when a factory chimney came into view I could no longer doubt.

At any rate we now knew where we were and it was the wrong place from which to round Lands End with a south-west wind. Tack- ing on and off we made no progress at all until ten o'clock that night when the wind shifted to west. With the change of wind the weather cleared, all the familiar lights came up, and at midnight we passed the

Longships and headed up Channel. Two days later, again at midnight, we were closing the Needles in clear weather with wind and tide both in our favour. A large passenger steamer outward bound, after clearing the Needles Channel, turned south and stopped, no doubt to drop the pilot. That done she incontinently turned west and rushed straight at us. Not wishing to gybe all standing I held on and she passed ahead of us within a biscuit's toss, as the saying goes, without even seeing us. At least no one on the bridge used a loud-hailer to blast us and the quiet of the night.

When my heart had stopped thumping we continued up the Needles channel, most of the crew gathered on the foredeck admiring the sights and the lights, while I sat happily steering, the wind dead aft and the boom squared off to starboard. The crew evidently assumed I had seen or heard the Warden buoy hidden behind the mainsail, for when they suddenly and simultaneously uttered a startled yell the tip of the boom was almost caressing the buoy as it slid by. Safely anchored off Lymington river to wait for daylight I had leisure to reflect on the varied perils that beset our coasts, while only the gentle clang of the pump reminded me of those we had escaped in Greenland waters.

Alongside next morning we set to work unloading and unrigging the ship. For yet another night the pump had to be manned but by the next day she had been hauled out. On stripping the lining in the galley it was found that water had been coming in at the damaged planks that Martin had thought were not cracked through. Insomuch as we had not reached Skjoldungen the voyage had been a failure. But it had been full of incident and we had all enjoyed it. Leigh Mallory's reputed answer to the question of why anyone should want to climb Everest—'Because it is there'—has been quoted *ad nauseam*. I should have thought that a better answer to that question or to why a man undertakes any adventure or enterprise is to be found in Stevenson's words: 'In the joy of the actors lies the sense of any action. That is the explanation, that the excuse.'

PART THREE

Heard Island, Southern Ocean

Patanela

November 1964—March 1965

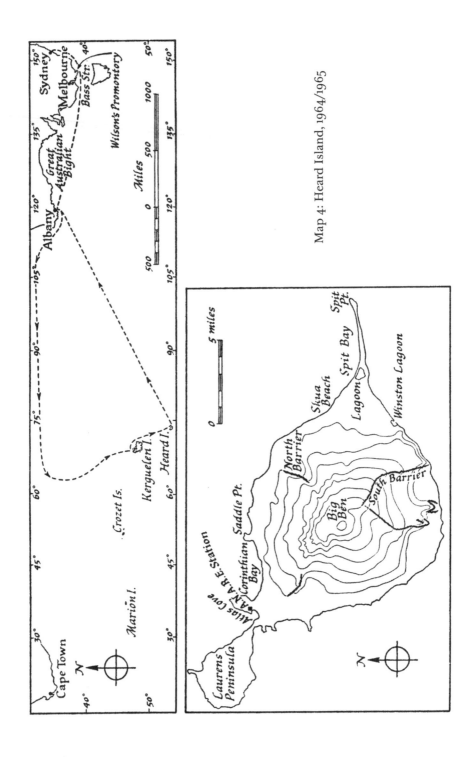

Map 4: Heard Island, 1964/1965

CHAPTER XIII

FITTING OUT

◆

HEARD ISLAND in Lat. 53° 10′ S. Long. 73° 35′ E., is an uninhabited sub-antarctic island lying about 300 miles to the south-east of the much larger island of Kerguelen. Measuring only some twenty-three miles by twelve miles it culminates in the peak known as Big Ben which is 9005 feet high. Thus the island is nearly all mountain, a mountain heavily glaciated on all sides; many of the glaciers terminate in ice cliffs that are washed by the sea.

As far back as 1957 I had had an eye to Big Ben but enquiries had shown that there was no safe anchorage where *Mischief* could be left. A letter, too, from Mr P. G. Law, then (and now) Director of the Australian Antarctic Division, had been discouraging. 'As regards your getting to Heard Island,' he had written, 'I cannot overstress the dangers which will face you if you proceed in a small boat. As you know, Heard Island is right in the track of the great westerly cyclones which sweep across the Southern Ocean with almost no intervening period of good weather of any duration. The seas are mountainous and altogether I can think of no worse place to sail small craft.' More than that, the lack of a safe anchorage meant that the boat, after dropping the shore party, would have to be sailed to Kerguelen where there are many good anchorages. With *Mischief*, with a crew of only six, I did not think this was on. It was the usual difficulty of being in two places at once. I myself would certainly want to land on Heard Island, and equally certainly I would not like to leave a reduced crew with the responsibility of navigating to Kerguelen and back again. I should have felt extreme anxiety both on their account and on my own, for if for some reason they had failed to return, the shore party would have been residents of Heard Island for a long time. From 1949 to 1954, when it was abandoned, Australia had maintained there a scientific base—huts, electric light, and hot baths—so perhaps we should not have been badly off. But in the end I decided to leave Big Ben for better men and went instead to Îles Crozet and Kerguelen. At least we went there at the second attempt, the first having ended when we suffered some storm damage, after which we had to be content with circumnavigating Africa.

In the winter of 1963/1964 I heard from Warwick Deacock, an ex-Army officer and a climber, then living in Australia, who was organising a private expedition to sail to Heard Island with the object, among others, of climbing Big Ben. *Patanela*, a 63-foot steel schooner, had been chartered for five months and he asked me to act as navigator, knowing that I had once been interested in Heard Island and had visited Kerguelen. A large amount of money had still to be found including £A8,000 for the charter. For several years *Patanela* had been employed in crayfishing in Bass Strait and the charter figure was based—oversanguinely, one thought—on the amount that could be made in a season's fishing. At that time the two owners and active managers of the boat, the Hunt brothers, were to have come with us. In the end they had to drop out and I was then asked to skipper *Patanela* as well as navigate. Since my experience had been limited entirely to sailing a small cutter, to be asked to take charge of a big, unknown schooner and an unknown crew was no light matter. Nevertheless, both the destination and the aims of the expedition were things after my own heart. After learning from an independent source in Australia that *Patanela* was a capable boat and in sound condition I did not long hesitate to accept. Arriving in Sydney on October 20th, more dead than alive after a long flight, I was met by Warwick Deacock and several members of the expedition. From the airport we went straight on board *Patanela*, then lying at the jetty of the Cruising Club of Australia who, besides allowing us to fit-out there, also allowed us to use the clubhouse. As is inevitably the way with a boat undergoing a major refit she was in a chaotic state, the deck almost impassable from the accumulation of junk. Work on her was not nearly so forward as I had expected and the chance of our leaving on the advertised date, November 1st, seemed to me remote. Apart from a mass of work below deck, all the running rigging had yet to be fitted, there were no cleats, nothing on which to hang rope-coils, no fittings on deck for sheet-blocks or tackles, and no binnacle.

Compared with the accommodation in *Mischief*, which is not luxurious, that in *Patanela* seemed to me only a little superior to what would have been found in a better-class slaver. Berths were needed for ten, a number that could not well be reduced. If five men were to be put ashore on Heard Island, we must have five left on board to work the ship. There were four good bunks in the fo'c'sle, the only snags there being that it was awkward to enter and pitch dark. An escape hatch on deck which would admit daylight, would normally be closed at sea. One entered it through a small steel door, after assuming a kneeling position on deck, and then climbed down a ladder backwards. I wondered where the remaining six were to be interred, and when our tour of inspection finally finished up aft in the small combined galley and saloon I was a little shaken when I learnt that this was the only remaining space. In here there were two spacious fore-and-aft bunks and the plan was that two should sleep side by side in each while the remaining two were somehow to be slung from the deckhead like bats. Where these six unfortunates were to stow their gear was a question that had also been left hanging—bat-like.

Being a bit of a cissy, I thought some other arrangement desirable. Amidships there was a huge hold, the cray-tank, that normally held seventeen tons of seawater and crayfish and had now been earmarked to carry 2000 gallons of fuel oil in drums. But the idea was to *sail* to Heard Island and we had space in the engine room for 1000 gallons of oil. I therefore suggested that we put only 1000 gallons in the cray-tank in the form of a single layer of drums on top of which we could build a temporary floor and four bunks. Like those in the fo'c'sle, the four men in the cray-tank would depend entirely upon electric light but they were better off in that being amidships they were in the steadiest part of the ship. Only the saloon-cum-galley had any daylight and the two bunks there, though uncomfortably wide, were obviously designed for the skipper and for the leader of the expedition. Nor would even they be exactly in clover. The floor space, measuring about nine feet by nine feet, contained a gas-stove and a sink, a table and two benches at which four could sit in discomfort; and at mealtimes, if not at other times, the whole crew, less the two men on watch, would be sitting or standing there. Washing, which at sea is admittedly an infrequent and possibly superfluous operation, would have to be done on deck with a bucket; there was no lavatory; and nowhere to hang or even dump wet oilskins except on the floor of the wheel-house. 'Conveniences', as Dr Johnson said, 'are never missed where they were never enjoyed.' Our crew of young, eager, resourceful Australians and New Zealanders, whose morale, I feared, might be affected by this too ungracious living, took it all in their stride, making light of deficiencies and of their gloomy quarters. The steel door of the fo'c'sle soon bore the legend 'Saloon and Bar'. Over the cray-tank door they painted 'All hope abandon etc.', and below, in lighter vein, 'Knock twice and ask for Maisie.' The galley-cum-saloon was labelled 'The Dirty Spoon', and the engine-room 'The Sauna'.

Warwick Deacock had undertaken to cook, the most onerous job on board, and manfully he performed his duties. 'All ills,' Sancho Panza used to say, 'are alleviated by food.' At sea, in ships more comfortable than *Patanela*, the ills can be many and various, and food becomes of supreme importance. Meals must be good, plentiful and punctual. On this store we were to have no complaints, we lived like princes. *Patanela* had a refrigerated hold which before we left had been stuffed full of steaks, chops, sides and shoulders of beef, mutton, pork, besides hundreds or thousands of meat pies, sausages, bacon, and eggs; and in Warwick we had a man born to grapple with these ingredients on a scale of the necessary grandeur. Thrice daily throughout the voyage he satisfied ten voracious appetites, his only relief coming on Sundays when the crew took it in turns to vie with each other and with the master in the splendour of their menus. The meat remained good throughout the voyage except for a side of beef that might have come from the Durham ox itself, a monumental piece of meat that became known to us as 'Mary', and which after we had been hacking at it for a few weeks, and making little impression, had to be thrown overboard. Nor, amidst this superfluity of solids, was drink lacking. We had each a can of beer every day, and spirits for high days and holidays.

But I am anticipating. Having seen the ship I felt it was no good teetering on the brink. Forthwith I unrolled my swag (we are now in Australia) and lived on board for the next five months. Young Douglas Hunt who unfortunately was not coming with us, gave us invaluable help during the fitting out and shared with me the rigours of living on board. The rigours were more severe then than they would be, I hoped, when we got to sea; but 'what does misery matter if we are all miserable together?' The small wheel-house aft through which one entered the saloon, the saloon itself, and the fo'c'sle, were being given a lining of special material to prevent condensation. In the various stages of this long process Doug Hunt and I lived like nomads, moving our bedding from the saloon to the fo'c'sle and back again two or three times. Cooking was out of the question. For breakfast we walked up to King's Cross, a sort of Australian Leicester Square, where an eating place remained open all night; we lunched on board off meat pies and beer, and after work went ashore for a meal at night.

Once the running rigging had been set up and the sails bent we could go for a sail in the harbour to see how they set and to mark the leads for the headsail sheets. But before that she needed more weight in her, so we motored up the harbour to the big Mobil oil depot where we received (gratis) 2000 gallons of oil, putting half in the engine room and half in the cray-tank. Some of our friends who knew we had gone to load oil were concerned when that afternoon a fire broke out in the depot, destroying storage tanks and doing £250,000 worth of damage. Fortunately we had left about an hour earlier. Manoeuvring *Patanela* to and from her berth at the Club jetty through lines of closely moored, expensive yachts was quite hair-raising. Doug Hunt handled her in masterly fashion and on one occasion, when she had to be slipped, he turned her in her own length. With her 160-h.p. Rolls Royce engine and big propeller she was in fact easy to handle once one got the hang of it. Unaccustomed as I was to wheel steering and to a boat of her size I was thankful to have Doug Hunt there from whom I could learn.

Patanela had been brought round from Melbourne to Sydney for fitting out by a scratch crew. Happily, at an early stage in the passage they had learnt to ignore the compass located in the steel wheel-house. On some points it was 50° out, more on others. There were two wheels, one mounted inside the wheel-house, the other on its outer side aft. From inside the wheel-house one could see very little, certainly not the sails, so that wheel was useless to us; and though the outside wheel was good for manoeuvring in harbour there was no place to put a binnacle and compass. So we took the wheel from inside and put it on deck abaft the mainmast where one could both see and steer, and connected it to the steering gear with a long shaft bracketed to the starboard side of the wheel-house. The tricky job of rigging this wheel with the necessary shafting and gear wheels was done by an engineering friend of the expedition. Indeed a great many hardworking friends with various skills rallied round to help us.

Having got the wheel in its new position we bought a binnacle for £30, lined it up fore and aft and fixed it to the deck. This left the wheel-house free for use as a chart-room where with a lot of bother we fitted a chart-table, a rack for charts, and a secure home for my sextant and chronometer watch. There is much to be said for steel yachts—strength, freedom from leaks, freedom from attacks by teredo worm—and in Australia, especially ocean racing yachts, more are built of steel than of wood. But in a steel boat small fittings such as these, or shelves for books and clothes, are not to be had by knocking in a few nails or screws. All deck fittings, too, such as ringbolts, have to be welded on or have a hole burnt for them. We carried a welding outfit on the voyage.

Meantime we were being badgered by the Australian Shipping Board who, with the professional distrust of amateurs, rather hoped to save us from our folly by preventing us from sailing at all. At their request we had to slip *Patanela* again in order that they could take measurements to work out her angle of heel. They did not regard our brand new suit of sails of the heaviest Dacron made as enough. We must have a spare suit made. Alternatively, as this might take a few months, we must carry enough cloth to make a suit ourselves. None of our navigation lights complied with the regulations and must be changed. And finally, the unkindest cut of all, we must sign on a certificated navigator as a spare in case I got washed overboard. Enough is enough. Warwick Deacock got himself elected a member of the Australian Cruising Club, had *Patanela* registered as a yacht, and from that secure ground told the Shipping Board, so to speak, to jump into the dock.

Not all the crew were available for work on board. Of those that were Ed Reid, who had spent seven years as radio operator in the Australian navy, was fully occupied installing our own transmitting and receiving set (on loan from the Army) in the engine room and rigging the aerial aloft. An engine room is not ideal for a radio but we had no other place to put it. Phil Temple, a writer and an entomologist, who had been on two New Guinea expeditions, was also busy with his own devices, rigging a string of outsize butterfly nets that could be hoisted to the cross-trees. When these were aloft it was hoped that any wind-borne insects on passage in our vicinity would be caught, thus providing food of a kind for scientific thought.

Later we were joined by John Crick, a young New Zealand student teacher, a climber with no sailing experience, black-browed and given to modern poetry, songs of the outback, sheep-shearing, Ned Kelly, and such like. Tony Hill was a young law student who might be described as debonair when he was not looking scruffy, though seldom quite so scruffy as Phil Temple or John Crick. He had done some sailing and soon proved active and able both on deck and aloft. He acted as mate and was of great help to me, competent, reliable, and able to jolly the crew along.

Two who were working all the time on the boat were coming with us only as far as Albany. Alec Theakston was busy mainly in the engine room, but he could turn his hand to most things and his ability as an acrobat might have come in useful later in the voyage. Jim McCormick, red-headed and consequently fiery, had a seaman's card and in our first days at sea his presence among a more or less inexperienced crew was more than welcome. He had sailed in the coastal trade and regaled us with stories of a full-blooded character, master of a trading schooner, known as the 'Beast of Bass Strait,' a nautical Jack Dempsey who, if provoked, would knock a man the length of the deck. The Beast had a less violent but equally unpleasant way of dealing with any man he found steering half a point off course by merely telling him not to bother to call his relief.

Members of the expedition who were still occupied with their own affairs used to come along in the evening to do some work. Dr Russell Pardoe (we had three doctors in the crew) had been twice to the Antarctic and had earned an M.B.E. for his work on those expeditions. Russ, as we called him, was quiet, thorough, and painstaking in everything he did, whether rigging lazy-guys or treating boils. His particular pets were two inflatable rafts for the landing party, together with their Johnson outboards. He brought, too, an aqualung which we were to have occasion to use. Colin Putt, our kingpin and sheet-anchor, was another New Zealander employed by Imperial Chemicals in Sydney. He was coming as engineer and climber, but he knew a great deal about boats and could make or improvise anything a boat might need. Any insoluble problems we had we left to him, a man of infinite resource and sagacity. It was mainly upon his advice that *Patanela* had been chartered.

Much hampered by visitors and press photographers the work gradually got done. The inevitable question of when we were going to sail could only be answered by 'When we were ready'. The junk on deck had now grown to mountainous proportions and had to be got rid of. Much as I, and others, enjoy throwing things overboard one can't indulge in that habit too freely in Sydney Harbour, or for that matter in any other. Finally all hands were turned on to make a grand clearance by carrying it all ashore whence Colin Putt took it away in a five-ton lorry. No one asked what he did with it. *Patanela* now began to look like a ship and we made arrangements to have the compass swung.

With the compass adjuster on board, a retired sea captain who had served in sail, we went up harbour beyond the bridge where we put the boat's head on various known bearings. Finally we spent a long time circling round a buoy. By this time the adjuster was obviously a worried man. He could neither account for nor correct the erratic behaviour of the compass. The magnets that corrected it for one bearing would make it hopelessly out on another. At the end of the long morning, dizzied by our circling of the buoy and the antics of the compass needle, and running short of magnets, our sea captain asked to be put ashore. He needed, he said, leisure to reflect, to think of something that he had not yet tried. On our way back it struck me that if his musings resulted in our having to find a new position for the binnacle, and hence the wheel, as seemed probable, we never would sail. I persuaded him, therefore, to give it another try and back we went under the bridge to repeat the morning's performance. The short interval that we had unwittingly allowed did the trick. To the surprise and delight of all the compass, having had time to settle down in its new surroundings, now behaved like a witch. The deviation on all points was slight.

As soon as we got back to the Club we announced that we would sail next day, November 5th. It meant working up to the last minute, the most essential job being the securing of three 100-gallon drums of water and some small drums of petrol which we were obliged to carry on deck. When the press photographers were at last satisfied, we cast off at 3 p.m. and as soon as we were clear started getting sail on. As we passed Sydney Heads we shook off the last of the following launches, streamed the log, and headed south with a good breeze at north-east.

CHAPTER XIV

TO ALBANY

———◆———

A LTHOUGH WE HAD STILL TO CALL at Albany to pick up three members of the expedition and to fill up with water and oil, the voyage had at last begun and we were heartily glad to be at sea. For my part I believed and hoped that the most worrying part of the expedition was behind us; for the next few months our only contentions would be with the elements. It is probably true of all such sea adventures that the stresses and strains are most felt while fitting out and if this has been thoroughly done there should be no need for worry during the voyage.

A thunderstorm soon killed the wind. Outside the Heads there was enough lop to give the boat some motion so that by nightfall the crew's joy at being at sea had begun to diminish. Warwick, who was among those afflicted with seasickness, characteristically refused to give in and dished up a stew for those feeling strong enough to eat. Nor were our invalids given much chance to recover. On the next day we had a head wind gusting up to Force 7 which at length obliged us to heave to, and a rare tussle we had dowsing the big mainsail with our crew of novices. She hove to very comfortably under the foresail alone, a tip I had had from *Patanela*'s original owner who had paid us a visit when fitting out.

We did not expect to enjoy much sailing on the 1800-mile passage to Albany. In November along the south coast of Australia fresh to strong westerly winds prevail and the current is also adverse. According to the Sailing Directions no sailing vessel leaving Sydney at this time of year should attempt to go west along the south coast of Australia. With our 160-h.p. engine we could afford to ignore this advice and indeed we had no choice, for the passage north-about would have been longer and more difficult. Moreover having started five days late we had no time in hand, so whenever the wind blew from forward of the beam we handed the sails and made full use of the engine.

Patanela off Sydney Heads

By the 8th we had rounded Gabo Island, the south-eastern extremity of Australia and about 240 miles from Sydney. For the first day or two the working of my sights produced some bizarre results. In working sights in the southern hemisphere east of Greenwich, as against in the northern hemisphere west of Greenwich, to which for the last four years I had been habituated, there are some small but important differences to be observed. Any neglect of these is bound to result in a nonsense. Fortunately, although the Australian coast is for the most part barren sandhills and scrub, without towns, villages, or even caravan parks, it is plentifully sprinkled with lighthouses. Thus by closing the land one could always verify one's position even if the lighthouse sighted was not the expected one.

After Gabo Island the next important landmark on the way round Australia is Wilson Promontory, the southernmost point of Australia in Lat. 38° 55′. When nearing it on November 10th in the teeth of a strong head-wind and short, steep seas, we went inshore to coast along the great, empty stretch of sand known as Ninety-Mile Beach where we had smoother water and less current. The weather report spoke of twenty-two-knot winds off the Promontory, so when Jim McCormick began hinting at the snappers that might be caught thereabouts, we decided to have a quiet night in Sealer's Cove in the lee of the Promontory. On the way we fell in with a shoal of barracouta. In a mad ten minutes Jim hauled them in as fast as he could free the hook to throw it in again for another to take. When he had caught fifteen, the fish stopped feeding as suddenly as they had begun. Having already caught and eaten a tunny we found the barracouta disappointing. They are all bones and the flavour hardly repays the trouble spent in eating them.

Sealer's Cove is a delightful anchorage surrounded by steep slopes of dense scrub and eucalyptus trees from which some enormous granite boulders stand out. Apart from the men in the lighthouse on Wilson Promontory there were probably no human beings within 50 miles, a pleasing thought for anyone familiar with our own crowded coasts. Possibly at the request of the Shipping Board, our bowsprit had been decorated with a terrible tubular steel pulpit extending its whole length. We were surprised it had stayed there so long. At Sydney I had made a rope net to hang between the bowsprit shrouds so we took the opportunity to cut the steel monster adrift. No tears were shed as it sank beneath the quiet waters of Sealer's Cove and its absence greatly improved *Patanela's* appearance. Warwick laid on an abundant meal and after lingering over cigars and whisky we set an anchor watch and spent a peaceful night.

The wind had dropped by morning. As we motored past Wilson Promontory in calm water we felt our wait had been justified. There is a deep, five-mile-wide channel between the cape and Rodondo Island, a magnificent, conical mass of granite 1100 feet high, an unmistakable seamark. Curiously enough, though the island lies so close to the shore of Victoria it is accounted as part of Tasmania. Cape Otway, which we passed next day, was the last land we should see for a week as we embarked on the long 1200-mile haul across the Great Australian Bight. More than anything, I think, the extent of the Bight made me fully aware of the size of this great southern continent. The Bight is reputedly stormy but we did not encounter anything much in the way of weather. Albert Rogers, our temporary engineer, worked with Imperial Chemicals in Sydney as an engineer and was thus taking a busman's holiday. Although he appeared to be enjoying it he was in a hurry to get back. Perhaps the heat of the 'Sauna' was too much, for he was a little on the stout side. So we gave him his head, the revolution counter shot up, and we went bumming along at seven knots, knocking off 170 miles a day. The racket was appalling, and the heat which Albert had to endure in the 'Sauna' increased accordingly. In addition, a big swell running made her roll heavily with no steadying sails. There can be no nastier or more wearing a way of getting about the ocean than motoring in a small boat.

On November 19th we began to close the land somewhere near Albany. When land appears at a distance the navigator is tempted to begin at once to identify various features. This is a mistake. The first surmises he makes are as often as not false and once made they are only grudgingly abandoned. On this occasion the nearer we drew the less I could reconcile my first ideas with the chart, and I had worked up quite a stew before we satisfactorily identified the lighthouse on Breaksea Island, when at once everything fell into place. Provided one has confidence—and it is a large proviso—it is easier to close a strange harbour at night when the lights are readily identified. Beyond Breaksea

Island we entered King George's Sound—discovered by Vancouver in 1791—and were soon in the dredged channel leading to Princess Royal Harbour.

No friendly launch came out to meet us as expected. At a loss where to go, we went alongside the vacant steamer wharf where we were soon found by a large body of friends and well-wishers. We had to move to a slightly dilapidated wooden jetty further up the harbour. Quite a crowd had assembled there, too, to watch us, and they did not assemble in vain. Our first attempt to come alongside nearly carried away part of the jetty and we spent what seemed to me like an hour going ahead and astern before we got safely berthed in the rather cramped space. There was a strong wind blowing but even so my handling of the ship must have been far from impressive. At that time of year Albany is a little too subject to strong westerly winds and though the harbour is surrounded by land its spaciousness allows the wind full scope. During our week's stay the wind blew almost daily and we delayed our departure by two days while a gale blew itself out. Lying at an open pile jetty broadside on to wind and sea we had often to let go all warps except the bow lines in order to ease the strain. When lying thus, head on to wind and sea, we had no more to worry about except the difficulty of getting ashore. The young and agile managed it by lying face down on the warp and hauling themselves across with an ankle hooked over the warp to steady them.

Once one had got ashore the rewards that Albany had to offer were meagre. Australian beer is strong and that is about all that can be said for it, while the pubs are bleak and tawdry to a degree, not unlike the dreariest of British Railways waiting rooms except that there is nowhere to sit and no coal fire. When it is not windswept the town of 10,000 inhabitants is pleasant and quiet, with an extremely wide main street, so wide that it has always a slightly deserted air. A kangaroo loped down it early one morning and instead of motor cars I half expected to see some mounted bushrangers. As Sir Fopling Flutter said of Hyde Park, 'Beyond, all is desert,' so beyond Albany township all is scrub. One has to motor many miles in order to see a farm. During our stay there only one ship entered the harbour. But this fine harbour was busy enough during the war and may in the future again be busy. This corner of Australia is now attracting attention and land once considered worthless is being taken up. Whaling, too, is carried on in a small way. There is a whaling station and the three catchers that serve it went to sea daily if the weather was reasonable. They had the assistance of a small seaplane spotter. The whales are on passage and are all taken on the continental shelf.

At Albany we were as free from formalities as if in Greenland. No Shipping Board would have worried us had we started from there. We made friends everywhere, were entertained officially and privately, and got all the help we needed. Colin Putt joined and eagerly took over the engine room from Albert. Dr Malcolm Hay joined, too, having just arrived from England where he had been to pass an examination in surgery. He took over our cine-camera. And lastly Dr Grahame Budd who had not been able to make the passage from Sydney. Thus with three doctors on board we were heavily over insured against illness and accident and, as is often the way, we suffered none. Grahame was an experienced mountaineer. Having been twice to Heard Island with A.N.A.R.E. expeditions he knew the island well, its peculiar weather, and the best way to tackle Big Ben.

On November 23rd we took on oil at the steamer wharf preparatory to leaving next day. As an expected spare sextant had not yet arrived and the wind was still at west we decided to wait. For the next two days we lay to our bow lines while a moderate gale blew, but by the 27th we were ready to go. Wishing to atone for our unseamanlike arrival we proposed to astonish the natives by sailing from the jetty without using the engine—an easy enough feat because we had only to hoist the staysail for the wind to blow her head round. As we let go aft the staysail was run up smartly and to our discomfiture came down no less smartly on the heads of the chaps hoisting, the strop on the block having come adrift.

With everything set we sailed down the narrow buoyed channel, on the point of gybing most of the time, while Malcolm Hay followed in a launch with the cine-camera. Sailing freely in the open waters of the Sound, *Patanela* no doubt made a fine picture which Malcolm seemed never to tire of taking. The launch buzzed around hither and thither, Malcolm busy with the camera, until a performance that had looked like going on for ever was suddenly cut short when Malcolm dropped the camera and dived, fully clothed, into the sea. Apparently the case of his exposure meter had fallen overboard. Having picked him up and said good-bye to those in the launch we made our last farewell of all to the pilot of the whale-spotting seaplane who came down close by and stood on top of his cabin to shout to us.

Outside the Sound we could steer no better than south by west, and next day, making little headway, we hove to. At Sydney we had been given a parachute anchor to try out, a thing that when folded took up less room than a bucket. After wetting it to prevent the wind taking charge, we shackled it to the anchor cable and dropped it in with about five fathoms of chain. When the 'chute had opened, which took a few minutes, we were surprised at the way this thirty-two-foot-diameter piece of silk held a boat of *Patanela*'s size and weight head to wind. Later, off Heard Island in a hard gale, when we hoped it would lessen the drift to leeward, the anchor held us for an hour until the enormous strain proved too much for the bronze fitting between the parachute cords and the cable shackle.

Contrary winds were almost a certainty until we had rounded Cape Leeuwin (Lat. 34° 22′ S.) and made some northing. We could not steer a direct course from Albany to Heard Island for this rhumb line course of about 2500 miles lay entirely through the region of the strong westerlies, the Roaring Forties. We planned to make our westing roughly in Lat. 33° S. where we might expect variable winds, in the so-called Horse Latitudes. On the 29th, with the engine assisting, we were some fifteen miles off the cape, making poor progress in a rough sea against a Force 6 wind. Violent squalls continued throughout the day. We seemed hardly to move, but by evening I was relieved to note that we were out of sight of land. This southwestern extremity of Australia was named by the captain of the Dutch vessel *Leeuwin* which rounded the cape as long ago as 1622. As with most capes at the extremities of continents the weather is often stormy, moreover reefs extend far out to sea and the current sets on to the land. It is a place that needs to be given a wide berth. As we drew north the weather improved and on December 1st we were doing five knots under all plain sail with a fresh south-east wind. Grahame, who had undertaken to make deep plankton hauls throughout the voyage, thought it time to make a start. Having rigged a boom and dropped the net and its two-cwt sinker over the side we discovered the electric winch was not powerful enough to haul it up. We had to be content to make surface hauls over the stern. It was not a popular pastime. The hauls had to be made after dark, several hands were needed, and our speed had to be reduced to two knots by shortening sail. The haul itself was the least trouble but the net had then to be taken forward to be hoisted on the staysail halyards, and the pump and hoses rigged for washing it down. However fine the weather, oilskins were the wear. The catch, sometimes as thick as minestrone, was bottled in preservative. In the past my own contributions to science, acting, of course, merely as a collector, have been few and grudging, none perhaps so grudging as this. But Grahame's enthusiasm or sense of duty were not to be withstood. Only if conditions were really bad could I bring myself to disappoint him and gladden the rest by refusing to allow a plankton haul.

Though in our chosen latitude we escaped having westerly winds, sometimes we had no wind at all. One windless spell lasted for three days, days when we had no qualms about using the engine. And we began to enjoy some really warm weather. I had not thought much of the weather at Sydney and at sea off the coast it had been like an English summer, wet, blustery, and not very warm. We began having our lunch on deck and Tony, who had brought a deck chair, could occasionally sit in it. On one of these calm, undeniably pleasant days, we stopped the engine for an hour for all hands to bathe.

Even with their occasional calms the Horse Latitudes, between the Trade Winds and the Westerlies, are pleasant to sail in. In the Trades one reels off the miles but the unvarying wind and weather become monotonous. Our changeable winds were interspersed with calms and our fine days with days of cloud and drizzle. Apart from the work of the ship we kept ourselves occupied. There were endless discussions about plans for Heard Island and for the prior landing we should have to make either at Amsterdam Island or Kerguelen in order to re-organise ourselves. As the voyage drew on these plans became settled and committed to paper, each man being given a particular responsibility. We had a more tedious occupation in the signing of several thousand postcards. A surprising number of people both in Australia and abroad had subscribed five shillings in return for which we undertook to send a postcard we had had printed signed by members of the expedition and stamped with an expedition stamp—an extension of the Polar Post racket.

Warwick thought up other ways of depriving the crew of sleep, the occupation that generally fills the leisure hours of most crews. Every Sunday someone inflicted a lecture upon his fellows, and beside this we had to furnish material for the ship's newspaper that John Crick had been told to edit. In time the first number of 'S.O.S.' appeared, the letters standing for 'Spirit of the Storm' which, I was told, is the meaning of *Patanela*, a Tasmanian aboriginal word. Needless to say there no longer are any of these, Tasmania having made a clean sweep of its aboriginals. The first number, amusingly illustrated by Ed Reid, proved to be the last. Though the material for it had been collected the second number never went to press as we were then too preoccupied.

Another calm day gave us the opportunity to empty and clean out the refrigerator hold which by then looked like an abandoned snow cave. Warwick and his helpers got half frozen as they worked inside sending up the food — and what masses there were!—before scraping off the accumulated ice, hosing down, and then baling out the water. By December 15th, having averaged about 100 miles a day mostly under sail, we were in the longitude of Amsterdam Island (Lat. 37° 40′ Long. 77° 30′) and about 180 miles north of it. There is a French meteorological station there and an anchorage of sorts. We had expected we might have to call there in order to transfer fuel from the cray-tank to the engine room bunkers, a job that could not be done at sea; but having used little fuel since Albany we decided to defer this until we reached Kerguelen. We had wind on most days and once we had turned south into the region of the westerlies we expected to have more than enough wind. Kerguelen is in Long. 70° E. and I did not intend turning southwards until we had reached Long. 65° E. a good two hundred miles to the west of it.

CHAPTER XV

TO KERGUELEN

—◆—

THE RUDE, INTEMPERATE SOUTHERN OCEAN is rich in bird life. Many more birds are seen here than in the Tropics, the Trades, or the Horse Latitudes. As we edged southwards so the bird-life increased. In our small world Russ Pardoe was the greatest living authority on sea birds and he recorded methodically all that were seen. The various kinds of albatross were the most common and the most to be admired for their majestic, effortless flight; when sitting upon the water they look a little gawky and stupid. The big wandering albatross, the sooty, the light-mantled sooty, the yellow-nosed, black-browed, and grey-headed, could all be seen, and could be identified if one was enough of a conjurer to follow a bird in flight through field-glasses while standing on a heaving deck. Shearwaters or mutton birds, petrels of many varie-ties, cape pigeons and prions, were always about. At night the latter were attracted by our stern light. Sometimes, looking aft at night, the prions were so numerous that one almost thought that large snowflakes were falling. The little storm petrels fluttering over and sometimes dancing upon the storm-tossed sea, no bigger than sparrows, and pos-sibly a thousand miles from the nearest land, seemed to epitomise gay courage and contempt for the worst the elements could do.

Any tendency to edge south too soon had to be resisted. On Decem-ber 19th when we were in the longitude of Kerguelen and 900 miles north of it in Lat. 35°, a strong westerly breeze led me to fear that we were already in the grip of the Westerlies. It proved a false alarm. After shifting north and then south, the wind stopped altogether. Four days later, having made all the westing we wanted (in fact we reached as far west as Long. 62° 30′), we shaped a course for Kerguelen. The weather soon became harder, the skies greyer, and the sea assumed that steely look which one associates with southern latitudes. Reefing and unreef-ing the mainsail, or lowering it altogether, became a daily and nightly occurrence. The main boom had no roller-reefing gear, in fact it had no reef fittings in the way of bee-blocks or sheaves. Moreover the after end was out of reach from the deck, being above the roof of the wheelhouse. Colin therefore bolted a block on the boom aft through which we rove a long rope from the clew earing forward to the mast so that several hands could tally on and haul the earing down to the boom by brute force. Since the boom had not to revolve we had fitted lazy guys, light lines from the topping lifts to the boom, which helped to prevent the sail from bellying out when being lowered in strong winds.

The weather was constantly boisterous but on the run down to Kerguelen we did not record any winds stronger than Force 7. December 24th was particularly boisterous, a day of vicious squalls. We reefed before breakfast, handed the mainsail soon after, and ran hard all day under foresail and headsails. At midnight hands were called to make sail, the wind having eased, and before turning in we hung up our Christmas stockings. Sure enough some seafaring Father Christmas boarded us in the early hours. After breakfast we displayed our various gifts and even smoked the cigars found among them. Our Christmas dinner we had decided to defer until lying in some snug anchorage at Kerguelen. A few days later, while Warwick was cooking breakfast, a big wave struck us and the resulting lurch flung him right across the saloon. He was cushioned to some extent by landing on me but he hurt his back and was out of action for that day. Except for the loss overboard of a lifebuoy we suffered no damage on deck. After this we built a strong pen round the stove for we could not afford to have the cook thrown about.

On December 31st, only some 150 miles from Kerguelen, we ran fast all day before a big following sea. At midnight most of us joined the watch on deck to see the New Year in with song and the ringing of bells, and early on January 1st, 1965, we sighted Îles Nuageuses at the north-west corner of Kerguelen. The surprise shown by the crew at this precise landfall was, I thought, a little uncalled for. Later we sighted the isolated rock Bligh's Cap, now called Ilot du Rendezvous, which is twelve miles north-west of Cap d'Estaing on the main island. The rock was named by Cook after William Bligh—'Breadfruit' Bligh of the Bounty—who was sailing master in the *Resolution* on Cook's third and last voyage. The discoverer of Kerguelen was not Cook but a Breton nobleman Kerguelen-Trémarac who sighted the island in 1772.

Thinking that he had discovered the great southern continent upon which the explorers and geographers at that time were so intent, Trémarac hurried home to report his discovery in glowing terms. Having merely sighted some land he rashly concluded that he had proved the generally held theory that there must be a large land mass in the southern hemisphere to balance the preponderance of land in the northern hemisphere. The next year, with three vessels, he was sent to explore the new continent which he had named South France. The smallness and the uselessness of his discovery soon became apparent and Tremarac had to sail home to acknowledge his mistake. There is a story that in his disappointment he renamed the island 'Desolation', but this is the name given to it by Cook when he visited it in 1776, unaware that it had been discovered four years before.

The island is about ninety miles long and its coastline is remarkable for the number of great bays and fjords reaching far inland, so much so that nowhere on the island is more than twelve miles from salt water. The eastern side is comparatively flat while the west is mountainous and has an ice cap of some extent known as Glacier Cook, the ice cap that two of us crossed when we were at Kerguelen in *Mischief* in 1960. From it several glaciers descend to the sea. The coast of Kerguelen was well known to the hundreds of whalers and sealers who visited it in the course of the last century. In 1843, for instance, there were said to be 500 such ships at work on the coast. But these men generally kept their own counsel. The first extensive hydrographic survey was by the French explorer J. B. Charcot in 1913–14, accompanied by Raymond Rallier du Baty. The latter had already spent a year on Kerguelen in 1908 when he sailed there with his brother and four Breton fishermen in the small ketch *J. B. Charcot*. Raymond du Baty's account of this voyage, *Fifteen Thousand Miles in a Ketch*, is one of the best sea adventure stories ever written. A striking thing about this book is that it was written in English and published in England and is unknown in France. In 1960 at the French base in Kerguelen no one had so much as heard of it. 'A prophet is not without honour, except in his own country.' One of my treasured possessions is an autographed copy of the book which I received very recently from Raymond du Baty himself.

Even as late as 1908 the big bay on the north coast known as Baie des Baleiniers was swarming with whales. In 1909 a French-Norwegian company established a whaling station at Port Jeanne d'Arc which was abandoned only in 1929. The island then relapsed into its normally deserted state until in the Second World War three German raiders used it as a base for raids upon shipping in the Indian Ocean. This incident, together with a realisation of the importance of the island as a weather station and possibly a future air base, stirred the French government into activity. In 1949 an expedition of fourteen men reconnoitred a site and in the following year a weather station and scientific base was installed. Port aux Frangais at the south-east end of the island has since increased both in size and scope. In the last three years complete surveys both of Kerguelen and Îles Crozet have been made and maps published.

Before leaving for Australia I had corresponded with the 'Bureau des Terres Australes et Antarctiques' in Paris to warn them that in the event of our not finding a safe anchorage at Heard Island we should like to bring *Patanela* to Port aux Français; which was, of course, agreed. But we did not want to go there before proceeding to Heard Island. What we wanted was a quiet anchorage, free from social distractions, where we could put in a couple of days hard work preparing the stores and equipment for landing on Heard Island. The place I had in mind was Baie du Recques, a few miles south of Christmas Harbour, and the last thing we wanted to see at that moment were Frenchmen, admirable hosts as they are.

Upon rounding Cap d'Estaing we could see the Bird Table, an unmistakable flat-topped mountain near Cook's Christmas Harbour. He had landed there on Christmas Day 1776 unaware that it had already been named Baie de l'Oiseau after the name of one of the frigates in Kerguelen-Trémarac's squadron. The *Antarctic Pilot* does not recommend Christmas Harbour and for that reason we avoided it: 'Good ground tackle is necessary as squalls blow with tremendous violence down the valley at the head of the harbour. In 1939 the *Bougainville* dragged her anchor while lying in this bay.' In 1840 Ross with *Erebus* and *Terror* had remained there from May to July carrying out magnetic observations. He called it a most dreary and disagreeable harbour and recorded gales on forty-five of the sixty-eight days he was there and only three without rain or snow. But that, of course, was in the southern winter.

Port aux Français, Kerguelen

South coast of Heard Island and Big Ben, from Spit Bay

We therefore carried on past the entrance to Christmas Harbour, admiring, as we went by, Pointe de l'Arche, a remarkable wall of rock originally forming an arch, though the top of the arch, the keystone as it were, has since collapsed. Suddenly, out of the blue, a helicopter appeared and proceeded to 'buzz' us. Were we being warned off or welcomed? And how did the French at Port aux Français, ninety miles away, whence we assumed the helicopter had come, know of our presence? Mulling over this strange happening we sailed on and turned into Baie du Recques where we met a strong headwind. It was late evening before we anchored in Ainsi du Jardin at the head of the fjord a cable's length off the shore. By then Warwick had our delayed Christmas dinner well under way and presently all ten of us squeezed into the saloon, overflowing up the steps leading to the wheel-house, to begin some serious eating and drinking—savoury, soup, roast beef and Yorkshire pudding, the whole screwed down by a monumental duff.

The mystery of the helicopter was resolved next morning when it appeared again high to the south and having spotted us landed nearby on an impossibly small, flat bit of ground. Russ who already had the rubber rafts in the water went to fetch off the five occupants. Only a fortnight before, a small summer base had been established at Christmas Harbour whence with the help of two helicopters a geological survey of the west end of the island was in hand. They had been as much astonished at the sight of *Patanela* sailing by as we had been by the helicopter, and they had expected us to see their two huts there and go in. We explained that we would be fully occupied for the next two days but promised to lunch with them the day we left.

Having watched our lively visitors soar into the air we went back to work. The bunks in the cray-tank had to be partially uprooted so that the oil from the drums underneath could be pumped into the main bunkers. Food and equipment for the shore party had to be broken out and made up into loads, and all the rigging overhauled. Thanks to a fine day we broke the back of the work. Overnight the weather changed. We woke to a day of rain and violent squalls and made the unwelcome discovery that we had dragged our anchor. The cliffs beyond the beach, down which a waterfall cascaded, which should have provided a good lee, merely acted as a wind shute. We anchored again as close to the shore as we dared, seeking to avoid the willy-waws which struck down from the cliffs whipping the water white.

Oiling having been finished and the cray-tank restored to order we wanted to erect the tents on shore and to give the eighteen-foot U.S.R. raft a trial run. Except that we were in sheltered water the weather conditions would make the trials realistic. The loaded raft with five on board went off down the fjord in search of rougher water. As I watched them through binoculars, the craft half hidden by spray as it bounced violently over the short waves, I felt relieved when they at last headed back for the ship. In the afternoon the wind still blowing and the rain hissing down, four of us took the raft to visit a wreck lying on the opposite shore. Besides satisfying our curiosity we wanted a few pieces of heavy timber. She had been a schooner, not much bigger than *Patanela*, the main mast in a tabernacle, and probably a Breton schooner judging by the word *St Malo* which could be read on the single cylinder Bollinder engine. The type of engine indicated that she had been built early in the century. She was for the most part buried in sand but we prised off some lengths of sound timber. Launching off in shallow water and breakers was a tricky business and at the first attempt we sheared off the pin of the propeller. Russ had a spare in the tool kit and when we finally got off we went back to the beach by the anchorage to see how the tent-erecting party were faring. One tent, one of these new-fangled, pole-less affairs, depending for rigidity upon being pumped up, might have been all right on the Lido but was obviously out of place on Heard Island or even Kerguelen. Inside the big pyramid tent, which we entered with difficulty through the sleeve entrance, we found a slightly disconsolate party sitting counting the drips. We had now only to water ship. Standing in the mouth of the stream below the waterfall we filled the U.S.R. raft by means of buckets; Russ then drove it back to the ship where they pumped the water out of the raft into the main tank. Finally the tents were struck, both rafts deflated and stowed, and we sat down to a well-earned supper, In two days, in spite of the vile weather on one of them, we had got the work done and were ready for Heard Island.

At Kerguelen fine days are few and perfect days are memorably rare. In 1960 on the ice cap we had enjoyed four such days in a row, days when the snow at 3000 feet turned to slush and when the reflected heat and glare almost brought us to a standstill. Now, on January 4th, when we visited the French at Christmas Harbour, we enjoyed another such day, calm, cloudless, warm. After waiting a bit to dry the tents we sailed at 10 a.m. and at noon motored past the rock arch into the harbour. At one or two places the steam rising from the drying ground had all the appearance of a hot spring. As our anchor went down two sportsmen paddled out to welcome us on a crazy raft of oil drums, while rockets, Verey lights, and cheers went up from the party on the beach. Confident that on this bright, windless day *Patanela* could safely be left, all hands went ashore in the rubber raft to make the tour of the base—two huts, two tents, two helicopters, and three wine barrels. A long table had been contrived outside and presently some twenty of us sat down to what the French—and we, too, for that matter—regarded as serious business. After some shots of cassis and *hors d'œuvres* we embarked on the main course, rabbit stewed in wine, cooked to such perfection that it might have been mistaken for chicken.

Rabbits are plentiful, too plentiful, on Kerguelen, as are sea elephants and several kinds of penguin. None of the latter shared our meal but a flock of skuas and sheathbills soon gathered round the table. One of the helicopter pilots, with a skill evidently born of long practice, caught a skua and administered what the French call a 'coup de Scotch'. The effect was remarkably sudden. Flying was out of the question, even standing became difficult, while the other skuas hungrily awaited its expected demise. Skuas, looking like ill-favoured scavenger crows, are not likeable birds, otherwise one could have been sorry for it. Towards four o'clock, for it had been a protracted lunch, both the weather and the guests showed signs of change, of impending dissolution. Once more we sang the *Marseillaise*, Grahame playing the accompaniment on his recorder while lying under the table, then arm-in-arm we went down to the beach, a swaying picture of international fellowship. The sails went up with a will, albeit a little raggedly, and as we swung round to face the entrance the oil drum raft launched off, more Verey lights soared up, and both helicopters took off to zoom dangerously round our masts. In gathering cloud we got clear of the coast before the wind died and left us tossing in a cross sea in rain and darkness.

CHAPTER XVI

HEARD ISLAND
AND PORT AUX FRANÇAIS

T HE STRONG NORTH-WEST WIND that presently got up enabled us next evening to round Cape Digby at the north-east corner of the island. There, on the lee side of the island, we had smooth water and ran fast all night down the east coast. By daylight Kerguelen was out of sight. The cold now became more appreciable, the sea temperature 39° F. and the air 43°, for we had now crossed what is called the Antarctic Convergence where there is an upwelling of cold water. At 8 a.m. of the 7th, fine, sunny, and windy, we were some ninety miles from Heard Island and early that afternoon, when we were still sixty miles away, we sighted Big Ben. There was no mistaking the characteristic lenticular cloud sitting over the summit and below it the glint of white snow slopes. That evening we sailed close by the McDonald Islands, three barren rocks, steep-to all round. No one has yet landed on them and it was in our minds to make an attempt. For this we needed a calm sea and the sea at this time was far from calm. The islands are some thirty miles west of Heard Island and in a freshening wind we ran towards it at five knots until midnight when we hove to about ten miles short of Winston Lagoon.

In 1962 the A.N.A.R.E. ship on its way to Mawson, the Australian Antarctic base, had landed on Heard Island a party of four which included Warwick Deacock and Grahame Budd. In the course of an attempt on Big Ben, after putting a camp at 4000 feet, they had been driven down by snow and gales. The route they had then taken, starting from Winston Lagoon, had appeared most promising, and on this account Winston Lagoon or its vicinity had been chosen as the place to put the present party ashore. Moreover, we entertained a faint hope that we might take *Patanela* into the lagoon itself where not only could a landing be easily made but where *Patanela* might safely remain while the party were on the mountain. There was no sheltered anchorage elsewhere. Even at Atlas Cove at the north-west end of the island where the Australians had their base, one would need to be in constant readiness to clear out at short notice.

By next morning the wind had died and except that the glass was falling conditions for a landing seemed fair. When we anchored in five fathoms about a quarter-mile off the lagoon the wind showed signs of stirring but fortunately from offshore. We had envisaged sending a raft in to the lagoon to take soundings but we had not to worry long about that. Even with the slight swell then running the water broke white right across the entrance, and seaward of the shingle spit that almost enclosed the lagoon huge boulders showed above the water. Both rafts were inflated and launched, one to be used as a stand-by rescue launch, and the loads got on deck. The breaking water on the bar discouraged any idea of taking even a raft in but west of the lagoon was a small beach where we could see some sea elephants and a penguin rookery. From the beach access could easily be had to the ridge called the South Barrier and so on to the mountain.

At that moment a raft might have got ashore but in order to establish the shore party for a month two trips would have to be made and the unloading and reloading would take some time. Before committing ourselves we waited a bit for the weather to declare its intentions. We did not have to wait long. The wind quickly rose to gale force. The strain on the cable proved too much for the electric winch so we got the anchor by hand and let the boat drift off shore. The wind had settled at north-west and when about a mile out we got the parachute anchor overboard in the hope of stopping or lessening the inevitable easterly drift. All along we had been at great pains to get to windward of the island and to stay there, to avoid at all costs having to beat back to recover it. The anchor held us almost stationary for nearly an hour until under the combined weight of wind and boat it gave way. The fitting between the anchor chain and the nylon parachute cords parted and although we re-rigged it with more shackles we finally had to haul it in and resign ourselves to drifting eastwards.

Hove to on the port tack we drifted to the south-east for the best part of two days until the wind moderated enough for us to begin motoring. A sight at noon of the 11th put us fifteen miles nearer the island than

Characteristic lenticular cloud over Heard Island (*Courtesy of Australia House*)

I expected, our total drift having been only about forty miles. Soon
we sighted the island and at the same time the wind increased again
to nearly gale force. But we had the island in sight and this time we
were determined not to let go of it. We plugged on until we had gained
the lee of the east side of the island and by evening were anchored off
the Gompton Glacier. Except that it afforded shelter from any wind
between north-west and south-west the anchorage had few charms.
True we could see the snow slopes and ridges of the mountain, but
shorewards, instead of a beach, we beheld merely black ice cliffs about
100 feet high. The Compton Glacier extends into the sea and owing to
the amount of debris it carries the ice is more black than white. To the
south of us, where is Spit Bay, we could make out the seas breaking on
the low gravel spit which extends seawards to the east for five miles.

This spit which protects Spit Bay and the east coast of the island
from southerly winds lay between us and Winston Lagoon. To round
it and reach the lagoon we had about twenty-five miles to go and in
order to be there in good time we started soon after 3 a.m. on the 12th.
Owing to the swell left by the recent strong winds the sea breaking on
the bar across the lagoon looked worse than it had three days before.
We anchored off the small beach while Warwick, who had to make the
decision, gazed long and earnestly at the surf. The decision made, no
time was lost in loading the raft and at 11 a.m. it started for the beach
with the five men of the shore party, Colin driving. In case of mishap
Russ stood by with the Zodiac raft which by now was less seaworthy
than one would wish. The rest of us watched their progress with anxiety as the heavily-laden craft vanished in the trough and reappeared
on the top of the swell. Soon we saw them stop outside the breakers to
await their opportunity. What happened in the few, critical moments
among the breakers we were too far off to see but we were heartily glad
when we next saw the raft being hauled up the beach.

Nearly an hour then elapsed before we were in contact with the
shore party and learnt how they had fared, both ship and shore party
being provided with 'Walky-Talky' sets. All had gone well until the raft
capsized in shallow water at the edge of the beach with three of the
party underneath it and the Johnson outboard still running. The load
had been well secured so that nothing was lost but a camera, and since
the party were wearing 'wet' suits they remained more or less warm in

spite of their ducking. Warwick added that the surf was then too bad to launch off for the second trip. We agreed to wait until evening in the hope that it might go down.

We saw them put the tents up high above the beach and then early in the afternoon we heard that they were about to launch. This they achieved and Warwick with Colin came off for the second load of stores. All went well on the second trip and by 4 p.m. the shore party were safely established with a month's food and we had squared up on board and were ready to go. Febuary 11th was the day appointed for our return. I wanted to pass round the west side of the island, a part we had not yet seen. But off Cape Lambeth only a mile to the west, the tents of the shore party still in view, we met a strong breeze while ahead of us stretched a long line of white water. No reef or spit lay in that direction, the water was being lashed by sudden and violent wind. We stood to the south to make an offing, handed the sails, and lay to under bare poles.

By next morning we were able to set the foresail and start sailing assisted by the engine. After a night of drifting we were not likely to fetch the west of the island and in due course the east coast showed up wide on our port bow. At noon, in bright sunshine we had Spit Point abeam. For the moment we were in calm water and in spite of being short-handed we hoisted all the sails hoping that the shore party would take note of this defiant gesture. A freshening wind soon made her too hard to hold. When the island disappeared that evening in a bank of fog we were once more under short canvas. Gales, sunshine, rain, and fog—we had had them all in the inside of a week. Happily, the vexed seas round Heard Island are free from ice and icebergs.

With a crew of five we had only one man on watch. Tony Hill, Russ Pardoe, Malcolm Hay, and I did two-hour watches, while Ed Reid who had the wireless to look after did the cooking. We missed Warwick. Ed positively liked food out of tins but he soon learnt to his dismay that his favourite, baked beans, was on the proscribed list. Ed's wireless transmissions, or attempted transmissions, took up a lot of time. We were a long way from anywhere, certainly too far from Australia to make contact. The news that the party had landed on Heard Island went by way of Mawson in the Antarctic. Some of his messages went by way of Cape Town and one by Singapore.

With Kerguelen lying 300 miles to the north-west, that is to wind-ward, I expected a hard passage. In fact, with moderate winds, and those generally from west or south of west, we had no trouble. On the evening of the third day we sighted Presqu'ile Monarch at the south-east end of the island and next day we were motoring against a strong head wind up the broad Baie de Morbihan. This bay has many rami-fications and Port aux Français, the French base, lies up in its north-eastern corner in what is probably the most exposed part. The bay is big enough to provide a long 'fetch' so that in a hard gale there may be waves two to three feet high outside Port aux Français. Its saving grace is a patch of kelp across the entrance, thus the small piece of water inside remains pretty smooth even in a gale. Since *Mischief*'s visit in 1960 three mooring buoys for three landing craft have been laid. There is therefore not much room left for anchoring and none at all for dragging.

We had timed our arrival to a nicety. When the 'Chef de Mission' came on board to welcome us he announced that lunch was on the table. Jeeps took us the few hundred yards from the little concrete jetty to the common messroom where the hundred-odd men and one woman who then comprised the base were already seated. Amidst a great wel-coming uproar of cheers and banging on the table we took our seats. We had an undeniably excellent meal, a meal such as only Frenchmen could produce on what is a desert island if you exclude innumerable rabbits and the quarter million sea elephants and a million penguins that inhabit the flat beaches of the east coast. I noticed my companions going at it hammer and tongs, Malcolm having a slight edge on the others, but to me it lacked the relish and refinement of our first meal here in 1960 when M. Perrimond presided over the cuisine. Or perhaps then, after the Spartan fare of *Mischief*, I was in a more appreciative mood than now after weeks of high living in *Patanela*.

As coffee was being served the whole assembly began chanting a refrain 'Cognac, Odot, Cognac Odot, Cognac!' I grasped the signifi-cance when after about five minutes of chanting M. Odot rose to his feet and produced his keys and presently the brandy began to circu-late. He was the quartermaster, intendant, or steward, a short, stout man with an imperial air, far more respectably dressed than anyone else. The chanting then began again: 'Cigar, Odot, cigar Odot, cigar!'

and once more M. Odot complied, and cigars were handed round. Perhaps the presence of guests made him more amenable. Once more the chanting broke out: 'Merci beaucoup, merci beaucoup, merci!'

After lunch we made a tour of the base, visiting the various huts where extremely intricate machines were ticking away day and night recording upon reams of paper whatever they were recording—obscure phenomena from the ionosphere or maybe the stratosphere. Their earnest, bearded attendants explained to me what each was doing. After the lunch we had had I was not in a receptive mood. My French being little and my knowledge of science less, I felt that they might as well have addressed their remarks to the moulting King penguin that I had observed standing forlorn and disconsolate by the flagstaff outside the messroom. Aided by the woman scientist who spoke some English I found the launching site for hydrogen balloons slightly more intelligible. While on our way in we had remarked the huge screen erected for protecting the balloons while being inflated and had mistaken it for a block of flats. In connection with the balloons, a mast seventy metres high was in process of erection, a considerable feat of engineering in view of the rocky ground and the force of the winds it had to withstand.

I was surprised at how few of the French, several of them very learned men, spoke any English, far more surprising than the fact that only one of us far-from-learned men spoke any French. Russ and Malcolm could sometimes be heard uttering what they thought might be French, but Tony who had spent a year studying in Paris spoke it pretty fluently and acted as interpreter. The base had expanded considerably since 1960 when the personnel numbered only seventy against 120, though we were told that in winter only about thirty are left there. And besides the new base at Christmas Harbour, a base had been established on Île de la Possession in the Crozet group at Baie du Navire, the anchorage where we had spent a fortnight in *Mischief*. I was told that a 'téléferique' now passed directly over the King penguin rookery through which we had so often fought our way—a piece of news that decided me to write off Baie du Navire as a place to be revisited.

Another change that had taken place was the closing down of the plant for extracting oil from sea elephants—they had, of course, first been slaughtered. This had been run by a private company which had permission to kill up to 2000 annually. The late manager of this, a tall, fair Frenchman speaking excellent English, known as the Viscount (and I believe he was a Viscount) was marooned at Port aux Français with neither instructions, money, nor even a passage home. We had thoughts of taking him to Australia but before we left we heard that a passage for him had been arranged.

We had arrived on a Saturday when they had their weekly film show. Before attending we went back on board to change our anchor. The Breton boatswain in charge of all the craft, a man who answered my ideas of a real Frenchman—black hair and moustache, red-faced, stout, with a very loud, hoarse voice—did not think our anchor man enough and loaned us a much heavier, stockless anchor. On this anchor we lay quietly enough till the Monday when I thought it time to move on. We had more than a fortnight to put in before our Heard Island rendezvous and did not wish to trespass for so long on French hospitality. On the Sunday they had insisted on our having all our meals ashore and for our part we had needed little pressing. As no doubt they would have done at home, they devoted Sunday to 'la chasse', most of the garrison setting out heavily armed and returning at dusk either with nothing or perhaps a scrawny rabbit.

With difficulty we persuaded the Chef de Mission and some of the hierarchy to visit us on board for drinks. In the end we mustered quite a crowd. Having given them all their 'coup de Scotch' I noticed they were not drinking very heartily and when I took a swig myself I understood why. I had given them whisky and sea water. While they were on board I explained to the Chef de Mission that we would like to spend some time at Port Jeanne d'Arc to which he agreed and at once began organising things to ensure our enjoying our stay there. From my point of view the chief attraction of Port Jeanne d'Arc lay in the fact that there was a vacant mooring buoy which we could use. Anchoring at Port aux Français was too much like anchoring at a place mentioned in an *Admiralty Pilot*, of which it remarks: 'Anchoring in this bight must be prompted by necessity and not by any hope of tranquillity.'

CHAPTER XVII

PORT JEANNE D'ARC,
HEARD ISLAND AND SYDNEY

O N THE MONDAY MORNING we found awaiting us on the quay a whole barrel of wine. I asked to be allowed to take only a couple of jerry-cans. We all liked our 'coups de rouge', or 'plonk' as the Australians called it, but I felt we would make little impression on a barrel. With us we had the Breton boatswain as pilot, three men whom we were to drop at Île Longue where the French run a flock of 700 sheep, and two climbers, both good chaps known to us as Jacques and Claude. They were to show us round Port Jeanne d'Arc and its neighbourhood.

We motored all the way, the trip taking about six hours, including an hour's delay at Île Longue to effect the relief of the shepherds. From this flock came the mutton we had been eating so heartily over the weekend, mutton that combined the sweetness of the mountain, the fat of the valley, and the tang of the saltings. According to our Breton friend the narrow pass at the north end of Île Longue contained mines. A German raider that had used Port Jeanne d'Arc during the war had laid them and they were reputedly still there. No one professed to believe seriously in these mines but I noticed that as we passed through the suspected area everyone on board gathered in the after part of the ship. We secured to the buoy at 6 p.m. and settled down to a cheerful evening entertaining our French guests.

The remains of the whaling station at Port Jeanne d'Arc that had been in use from 1909 to 1929 are still substantial—huge wooden flensing platforms, whale-boats, boilers, vats, storage tanks, a wooded jetty with a light railway, blacksmith's shop, carpenter's shop, and two separate barracks. Part of the barracks are still habitable and are used by the French who, during the season of winter gales, launch their hydrogen balloons from Port Jeanne d'Arc instead of from Port aux Français.

Thus the balloons have a chance of gaining height before passing over Port aux Français 20 miles to leeward. The helicopter arrived next morning to take back the Breton boatswain and to allow the Chef de Mission to inspect Port Jeanne d'Arc. Meantime Claude and Jacques had established themselves in the barracks and were busy cooking lunch for us. Quite rightly they believed in living on the country. They had shot a rabbit in the doorway and had a big pot of mussels boiling over a fire outside. They had brought bread with them and the barracks kitchen was fully stocked with tinned food and a barrel of wine.

In the afternoon we walked up Dome Rouge (1150 feet), a bare stony ridge where winter snow still lay in drifts. Returning by the shore of the fjord we put up some duck and a brace of these rather scraggy birds was duly shot for supper. We came upon some sea elephants enjoying their two or three months' repose and a few stray King penguins. This handsome bird, next in size to the Emperor penguin, with blueish grey back and white breast, has a bright orange patch on the side of the head merging with a similar band at the neck. The two Frenchmen and three of us were to make an excursion to the lower slopes of Mt Ross (6430 feet) the highest peak of Kerguelen. Claude and Jacques talked of starting at 4 a.m. but in the course of the evening, helped by some 'coups de Scotch' they became more reasonable. Russ, Malcolm and Ed went off to the ship to pack their rucksacks before returning ashore where they were to sleep. For ship-to-shore transport we had now only a two-man rubber dinghy so that the ferrying business took some time. It was long after midnight before Tony and I got back on board.

We did not rise very early, nevertheless, as I had suspected, we were in time to see the climbing party shoulder its burdens and slouch off. Two days later they returned, very late in the evening and tired. They slept at the barracks where Tony and I most unwisely joined them for a continental breakfast. Coffee and rolls are very well, but we found them drinking Ovomaltine and eating sweet cake. This was not only revolting but annoying because we now had fresh bread on board. With our gas oven and some dried yeast it had been simple enough to make. I rather fancy myself as a master baker but Malcolm, fired by my example, soon took it out of my hands, and began turning out better bread and in addition spice buns. With only five on board baking need not be quite incessant. Henceforth, until we had re-embarked the shore party, we enjoyed bread every day.

The following Saturday a landing craft brought a large party of visitors including two more climbers. With them, Tony and Malcolm left that afternoon to have a look at Mt Ross. Tempted though I was I did not feel happy about leaving the ship. We had had one hard blow on a day when Tony and I had been ashore separately. Arriving back first I had been horrified to see the staysail, which had not been properly secured, flapping madly halfway up the stay. The rubber dinghy had not blown away, for we always weighted it down with stones, but having paddled a short way out I came back. There seemed to me to be every chance of missing the ship and being blown down the fjord, or of grabbing the ship and losing the dinghy. The line which we had rigged between ship and shore in anticipation of such happenings had been submerged in kelp. Even when Tony came back we had to wait for the fiercest squalls to subside before we could go on board to secure the sail.

On a fine, clear day I went a long walk to the head of Baie Swain whence Mt Ross showed up well. There are two summits to this fine snow peak, the smaller appearing fairly simple and the main peak extremely difficult. I met several elephant seals and King penguins. The latter seemed to be moulting and in that state preferred the company of a sea elephant to that of their fellows. A sea elephant lay in a mud wallow, only its eyes and mouth showing, while a King penguin stood a foot from its mouth in deep meditation. On the way back I approached this sea elephant to stir it up, and when it opened its mouth wide and bellowed so ferociously that involuntarily I started back, the penguin never so much as moved.

The climbing party were away four days during which Russ, Ed, and I amused ourselves cooking, collecting mussels, baking bread, and playing chess. Grahame had taken his pocket chess set with him but Ed had carved some pieces with which we had a lot of fun. We were all much in the same class, a pretty low class, and defeats were not taken to heart. On January 31st the landing craft came to retrieve the Frenchmen and on the following day we ourselves set out for Port aux Français. It was already blowing very hard as we approached the anchorage where, we had been told, there was now a vacant buoy, one of the landing craft having been slipped for repairs. Three times we tried and failed to pass a warp through the shackle on the buoy, the wind increasing all the time. Rather than anchor there I thought we should be safer in the lee of Point Molloy a few miles away. There is a hut there and two leading lights to show the anchorage. We set an anchor watch. In the course of the night the gale increased and both the land and the light became obscured in pitch blackness. It was therefore difficult to tell whether or not we were holding. At 4 a.m. a resounding bang on the keel brought all hands on deck with a rush. We were close inshore among kelp. Within a minute we had the engine going and after a few more bumps got into deeper water. We motored back under the Point, dropped anchor, and at once drifted away fast, the wind blowing as hard as ever. Three times we anchored in different places and each time the anchor wrapped itself in kelp on the way down and failed to hold. At the fourth attempt we succeeded.

We remained there while the wind blew itself out and on the next day secured to the buoy at Port aux Français where we learnt that during the gale gusts of Force 10 had been registered. Using his aqualung Russ examined our hull and reported no damage. We dined ashore, watched an amusing film of life at the base, and agreed to have lunch ashore next day before sailing for Heard Island. It was another windy day. The confidence that we had expressed at lunch and had still felt as we went down to the quay, had waned by the time we climbed on board. The Breton boatman took us off, and in spite of the comparative calm behind the sheltering kelp we had a job getting ourselves and our belongings—gifts of food and drink—from the launch on to *Patanela*. To leave in such conditions, when a failure of the engine or a mistake in casting off would at once put us in danger of hitting a landing craft or the rocky beach, seemed unwise and was not necessary. We still had six days in which to reach Heard Island. We waited, and in consequence spent another anxious night. How I wished we had been safely at sea instead of lying to a buoy in cramped surroundings with a gale blowing! It seemed to blow harder than it had two nights before and here we had no sheltering land close to windward. We doubled the chain to the buoy and remained on deck though we could do little except pray that the buoy would not budge. At 3 a.m., when the wind showed signs of moderating, we turned in.

After a late breakfast we sailed and went so fast that by noon next day we had only 150 miles to go. We hove to that night and remained hove to all next day while it blew hard from northeast, the barometer high and steady at 29.5. On the 8th we were drawing near the island and since we preferred to be at sea rather than at some uneasy anchorage we hove to well west of the McDonald Islands. Early next morning we let draw in a rough sea and high wind at south-west. As we closed the northwest end of the island the weather became more violent, squalls accompanied by sleet and rain lashing us in rapid succession. Under bare poles, chased by huge following seas, we shot past Red Island at three knots. Atlas Cove and Corinthian Bay, two of Heard Island's supposedly better anchorages, were mere sheets of foam where frequent willy-waws swept the water high into the air. It was a boisterous welcome.

Once past Rogers Head we could set the staysail but not until we were off Compton Glacier did we find any sort of a lee. Further round still we went to anchor off Skua Beach in Spit Bay in seven fathoms. Although on the next day, February 10th, we would be a day ahead of schedule we did not think the shore party would take it amiss if we gave them the chance to come off. Accordingly we started at 6 a.m. to motor round the Spit to the landing beach. We were relieved to see the tents there and at length a moving figure, though it seemed to us that they took our arrival very calmly. In fact it created so little stir that we began to wonder if they were all there or even all alive. After a tense hour Warwick came on the air and we listened in awe-struck silence to a remarkable bulletin. He had not forgotten his army training: 'Shore party to *Patanela*, Shore party to *Patanela* [could it be anyone else?]; the ascent of Big Ben has been accomplished; all the aims of the expedition have been achieved.' Whereupon Tony grabbed the set from Ed and asked Warwick to give us his news in Australian.

All the party were well and all five had stood on top of Big Ben. This was what we wanted to hear. Meantime they were more than ready to come off but the surf was bad. We said we would wait until 6 p.m. We should have to go back to Spit Bay to anchor and wanted to round the Spit before dark. I doubt if the surf had gone down much when at 5 p.m. they decided to try. Of course by next day the surf might have been as bad or worse, nevertheless, looking back, I regret that we did arrive a day early. The fact that we were there waiting no doubt persuaded them to try when conditions were not good enough. They got off without mishap but at the cost of leaving behind all personal gear and all the expensive equipment. They had climbed Big Ben but I felt that the island had had the last word.

Late that evening we got under way and headed south to clear the Spit. The ice of Winston glacier, its black moraine, and the little landing beach below, faded in the gathering gloom as we drew rapidly away, leaving Heard Island to relapse into its customary solitude. A solitude that seems unlikely to be broken for some time, for now that the mountain has been climbed there is little left to be done. Great is the incentive of profit but even if the elephant seals again become plentiful there, I doubt if in these days of ease anyone would be found willing to emulate the men who sailed to Heard Island a hundred years ago. In ships not much bigger than *Patanela*, men returned to this forbidding island year after year as a matter of course; when small parties would leave the comparative comfort of their ships to live on the beaches for six months or even a year in rough huts built of stones and bits of driftwood, cold, squalid, subsisting on seal meat and blubber like so many castaways.

The following notes on the sealers of last century have been sent me by my friend Mr Barnes, curator at the Mariners Museum, Newport News.

The *Roman*, 350 tons, sailed from New London on June 24th, 1870, to Heard Island and returned May 3rd, 1871, with 1500 barrels of sea elephant oil. She sailed again on June 26th the same year and returned June 9th, 1872, with another 1518 barrels, as well as 21 barrels of sperm oil. Her third voyage from July 16th, 1872, to March 31st, 1873, resulted in 1225 barrels of oil, and on a fourth voyage from May, 1873, to April, 1874, she again brought back 1440 barrels of sea elephant oil and some whale bone.

A smaller vessel, the schooner *Roswell King*, 97 tons, sailed from New London on June 29th, 1870, for Heard Island and returned with 1750 barrels of sea elephant oil on April 26th, 1873. She sailed again on August 5th, 1873, and returned April 29th, 1875, with only 55 barrels.

Sir Joseph Hooker, referring to his landing on Heard Island in 1842 when he was on Sir James Ross's Antarctic expedition as bota- nist, wrote: 'We saw six sealers; two were Americans and two Portu- guese from the Cape Verde Islands. They were left on the island by the whaling vessels we met with at Kerguelen, their duty to hunt sea elephants. The men engaged to remain three years on the island, and see the whale ships only for a short time in the spring of the year.'

A naturalist on the *Challenger* expedition 1872–1876 wrote: 'There are said to be 40 men on Heard Island. Men occasionally get lost upon the glaciers. Sometimes a man gets desperate from being in so miserable a place, and one whaler that we met at Kerguelen said, after he had had some rum, that occasionally men had to be shot: a statement which may be true or false, but which expresses at all events the feeling of the men. But they had good clothing and did not look particularly dirty. They lived in wooden huts, or rather under roofs built over holes in the ground. Around the huts were oil casks and a hand barrow for wheeling blubber about. Their principal food was penguins and they used penguin skins with the fat on for fuel. Captain Nares saw five such skins piled on the fire one after the other.'

Our castaways looked none the worse for their month on the island, though we gathered that it had not been altogether a picnic. Having established a camp at 4000 feet they waited for several days for a quiet spell, determined to do the remaining 5000 feet in one jump. When their chance came they started very early and were all on top by midday, but they had hardly had time to look around and to examine the crater (Big Ben is a volcanic mountain) when the weather broke with its cus- tomary suddenness. In wind and driving snow they had had some dif- ficulty in finding their way down. Besides climbing the mountain they had spent time surveying, collecting, and making counts of the sea ele- phant and penguin colonies—colonies that are recovering but slowly from the ravages inflicted by the sealers of the previous century.

In the first week after leaving the island we ran over 1000 miles. Homeward bound, with a good ship under us, we did not care how hard the following gale. Even when under only staysail and foresail she reeled off the miles and if the gale moderated we hoisted the reefed mainsail. On February 14th the crew obstinately refused to let me stand my watches (it was the skipper's birthday), and to have all night in at sea is about as nice a present as a man could wish. By the 20th we were already up to Lat. 41° S. and the brave westerlies showed signs of faltering. Indeed, on the next day when still 500 miles out from Albany we were reduced to motoring—but not for long. We stopped the engine for all hands to bathe and we had lunch again on deck.

Two days later, eighteen days out from Heard Island, we picked up the Eclipse Island light and early that morning were fast alongside at our old berth at Albany. After taking on oil and water we sailed next day for Sydney. We were in a hurry. Having never taken part in ocean racing, and having generally preferred comfort to speed when cruising, I found it a salutary experience to be asked to make Sydney in thirteen days. In common with most expeditions nowadays we were under obligations to the press and it was at the request of *The Australian* newspaper that we aimed to be off Sydney Heads at 9 a.m. on March 14th, a Sunday. By using the engine we could do it easily but there were limits to what we were prepared to endure and we hoped to be able to sail most of the time.

We made good progress across the Bight until on March 5th, during a heavy squall, when we were trying to reef, something let go with a bang. At first I thought the mainsail had split. Having got the sail down we discovered that a lug at the foremast head holding up the starboard shrouds had broken. We had to lower all but the staysail, yet so strong was the wind that we did four knots for the rest of the day and part of the night. Three days later we put into Portland behind Cape Wilson and anchored in the roads. We put a length of chain round the masthead to which we shackled the shrouds, and at the same time transferred seven drums of fuel from the cray-tank to the bunkers. At this point we had logged 10,000 miles and we took time off to celebrate this with a superlative curry before getting under way again at 10 p.m.

The next night we passed Wilson's Promontory. Although the night was clear and cloudless the smoke from bush fires then raging in south and south-eastern parts of Australia made the lights difficult to spot at even half their normal range. Having passed Gabo Island and turned north we lost the wind and for the first time in the voyage the engine chose to misbehave. The thermostat stopped working and everything came to the boil. It seemed highly probable that the reception committee off Sydney Heads were going to be disappointed but at that moment a breeze made itself felt and rapidly strengthened. Soon we were fairly romping up the coast.

We arrived off the Heads two hours two soon and jilled about until some launches appeared when we went in and met them. This time a berth had been arranged for us at the Motor Yacht Club, a club with magnificent premises and a slightly decrepit jetty which I nearly knocked for six on coming alongside. Among the welcoming and admiring crowd—their admiration no doubt diminished by this unseamanlike finish to the voyage—were the owners of *Patanela*, the Hunt brothers, delighted to see her back and to have such good accounts of her from us.

In his famous description of a prize fight Hazlitt summed it up as 'a complete thing'. In my opinion, devoted as I am to both sea and mountains, to sailing and climbing, this expedition deserves to be so described. A long voyage, much of it in unfrequented waters, and at the end of it a remote, uninhabited island crowned with an unclimbed mountain. It was an enterprise that needed to be undertaken, one that I myself had shrunk from attempting, and that now, thanks to Warwick Deacock's initiative and drive, had at last been accomplished. From first to last we had been a happy party, each man pulling his full weight. I may have regretted not to have set foot even on Heard Island, much less on Big Ben, but that was implicit in the job I undertook. Besides enjoying every minute of it, I considered it a great privilege to be skipper of so fine a vessel and to sail with so eager, lively, and resolute a crew.

PART FOUR

◆

East Greenland, Return Engagement
Mischief

June–September 1965

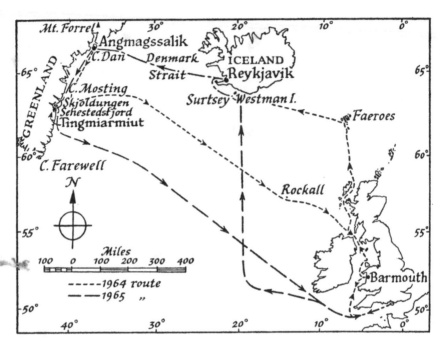

Map 5: East Greenland, 1964 and 1965

CHAPTER XVIII

TO ICELAND

———◆———

T EMPTING THOUGH IT WAS to spend a month or two seeing Australia and New Zealand, I had at the back of my mind the thought of a return match with East Greenland. Defeat rankles. Our failure to reach our objective there in 1964 was reason enough for having another go in 1965. Having seen *Patanela* unloaded, cleaned up, and back in her owner's hands, I came home before the end of March in time to begin scratching around for a crew. 'Strenuousness is the immortal path,' as some sage has observed, 'sloth is the way of death.'

While on a quick visit to Lymington to inspect *Mischief* and to take home some of her rigging for overhaul, I had an assurance from 'Noddy' Wareham who had been with us the previous year, that he would like to come again. Then I had a letter from R. Bradley, a stranger, who hinted that he might be rash enough to volunteer. He kept a day-boat on the east coast and had a longing to make a deep-sea voyage. Like me he was well stricken in years and though at one time he had been a long distance cyclist he was no longer in racing trim. In view of this and the weight of *Mischief*'s gear he was not really up to work on deck and offered to come as cook. 'When they bring you the heifer be ready with the rope,' as I have quoted before. I took Bradley to Lymington to look at the boat and when we parted he said he would think about it. I therefore expected a refusal and was agreeably surprised when he wrote to say that he would come.

Brian Hill, a young man from Weymouth, I acquired through a friend of a friend. No stranger to the sea, he had worked as a hand on a small tug on a delivery voyage to South America; moreover, he left me in no doubt, as some do, that he really meant business. I hoped to start towards the end of June a month later than usual, the idea being that by the time we arrived off East Greenland ice conditions were likely to be easier. On another visit to Lymington in mid-May, when I still had only these three starters, I had an offer from Brian Thomas, a young shipwright apprentice in the boatyard. He was as strong as an ox and altogether a likely looking chap. These inroads of mine on the labour force of the Berthon Boatyard were not altogether welcome. It was not until the end of May, when I was becoming agitated, that I knew for certain that he and Noddy would both get leave.

As often happens, in the last week or so I had several offers and finally picked Brian Holloway (the third Brian), a young, footloose New Zealander. Many young people from overseas come to England to see Europe, to make the modern equivalent of the Grand Tour, very much on the cheap. They work at various odd jobs merely to make enough money to travel about. Young Holloway seemed to be living mainly on charm and hope. In a small van, accompanied by two girls and a cat, he called on me at Barmouth on the way back from a tour of Scotland. He had no commitments—except subsequently to one of the girls—and had cruised in a yacht from New Zealand to the South Sea islands, so I took him on, hoping he would prove as good as the New Zealanders we had had in *Patanela*. He was, besides the only one of the five who looked like being of use on a mountain. I had no climber. One whom I had hoped would be coming had been unable to make up his mind. Brian Holloway had done a lot of skiing but no mountaineering. The previous year, when we had three climbers on board, we had failed to reach our mountains, so that for a man who wanted to climb the prospects were too uncertain.

We began fitting out about June 14th and had to work hard to be ready by June 25th. The weather hindered us and neither Noddy nor Brian Thomas were immediately available. In the end we missed the morning tide of the 25th, having to wait for a reconditioned cabin heater to be installed, and for the Customs, our authority to draw bonded stores having been delayed. We were not sorry. For some days the shipping forecasts had been uniformly depressing, nothing but strong westerly winds and rain. Towards evening the weather seemed to improve a little and we decided to go. Accordingly at 5.30 p.m. in drizzle and a fresh south-west wind, we cast off and motored down the river. Having hoisted sail and made one board across the Solent in which we lost a little ground, I decided to anchor for the night in Yarmouth roads. With a strange crew, most of whom would probably be seasick, it would be no fun beating out at night into the Channel. At least we had made a start.

By morning the rain had stopped and the wind moderated. At 8 a.m. we got our anchor and beat out past the Needles in good time to avoid being overrun by the two hundred-odd yachts setting out on the race round the island whose sails we could see far astern. So much for our departure as I saw it. But a friend, Mr W. G. Lee of Lymington, who observed it narrowly from Hurst Point, who shares my romantic notions of the sea and is better able to describe them, saw it thus:

Mischief moved slowly away from her anchorage into the fairway while a figure twice clambered out on to the bowsprit. She headed up into the freshening breeze while the jib was hoisted. Then the gaff could be seen to lift with the mainsail following, and with these sails set *Mischief* moved away on the port tack. After ten minutes or so she went about and beat across towards Yarmouth and then returned on a long tack to the Pennington side of the channel. I feared she was, in fact, putting back into Lymington for some reason, but eventually she went about again and thus confirmed her intention of putting to sea. Now on the starboard tack she sailed right across under the Island shore west of Sconce Point and made quite a bit of ground, but the next tack was across the last of the flood tide through the Narrows and she barely made any progress before finding herself close in under Hurst Point. Here she went about again, close under my position on the beach, to make a long beat through the narrow channel. Major Tilman was clearly visible at the helm and four of the crew on deck. A dark clad figure made his way out on the bowsprit as *Mischief*, meeting her first waves, plunged and reared a few times to remind him of his position.

She carried this tack past the NE. Shingles buoy and passed inshore of the Warden buoy. It was now clear that the second head-sail was due to go on, but there seemed to be some difficulty because Major Tilman left the helm and went forward to help. Meanwhile *Mischief* was forging ahead towards an inhospitable lee shore between Totland and Alum Bay. Then the bunt of the headsail could be seen and the ship bore off temporarily, as I thought, to free the sail in some way, but in the process heading directly inshore as though a novel ascent of Tennyson Down was intended. After a somewhat agonising interval (at least for the observer from the other shore whose binoculars foreshortened the distance to give an entirely false impression) the second headsail went up and *Mischief* went about to stand into the regular channel.

All the time the wind was freshening and was such at Hurst Point that I could not keep my eye to my camera viewfinder for more than a few seconds before it watered intolerably and left me to guess what was in view. After one more tack inshore *Mischief* went away on a long tack to clear the Needles. As she beat out into the shipping lane the sea around and ahead was visibly rougher with a lot of white showing over the Shingle shoals. Near the Middle Shingles buoy she came on to the starboard tack which let the sun show off the full curve of her main, and showed up her headsails as taut triangles of light. Sailing thus on the horizon with her gaff rig and headsails emphasised, she reminded me of a nineteenth-century print—a lovely sight but a bit too distant to appreciate with the unaided eye.

On this tack she cleared the Needles but the glasses showed it to be an exciting stage of the passage, for where the seas lifted over the shoal between the Bridge buoy and the Island they were steep and confused. I clearly saw *Mischief*'s forefoot rise high in the air time and time again, and then her stern and counter as she plunged and lifted until she passed behind the lighthouse. In due course I caught sight of her again, hull down, but with her gaff still discernible, making hard progress due south, getting little help from the strong south-wester and none as yet from the west-going tide. And so I watched until it became a strain to see her at all and the time had come to turn for home. As I did so I casually glanced eastwards along the Solent and an amazing sight presented itself. It was as though a barricade had been thrown across the whole width from Bouldnor to the Beaulieu river as the two hundred and fifty yachts participating in the Round-the-Island race beat out towards Hurst and the Needles Channel. I became aware, too, of quite a crowd having collected along the beach. So here I was, at the crossroads, so to speak.

On the one hand I had a fleet in which teak and mahogany, nylon and terylene, glassfibre, tufnol, polyurethane, stainless steel, titanium, radio D.F., echo sounders, remote reading anemometers, sophisticated electronics and all that ingenuity has yet devised, being harnessed for a circuit of the Isle of Wight, while hull down on the other hand was a 1906 working cutter with flax canvas, wooden blocks, hot dipped fittings, tarred seizings and Scotsmen in her rigging, and thousands of sea miles behind her, bound for the ice floes of East Greenland. I wondered how many, if any, of the now swollen crowd, knew or cared. It may be that in one sense I was still as alone at Hurst Point as I had been nearly five hours ago. Curiosity held me there while the leading yachts came through, but I had made my choice, and with scarcely a glance at the approaching fleet I walked back along the shingle spit well rewarded for my morning vigil.

Outside the Needles the sea was still rough enough to make a camera of mine, kept on a shelf above my bunk, jump off, find its way way out of the cabin, to finish up in the bilge near the engine. This bath in a mixture of oil and sea water did it no good, but I had another camera with which I could take black-and-white photographs. Brad, the cook, and Brian Hill quickly succumbed, and Kiwi, as we now called Brian Holloway, cooked our supper. Three Brians on board were too many. Brian Thomas, who came from South Wales, we renamed, with great originality, Taffy.

Early on the afternoon of the 29th we passed the Wolf rock where a Trinity House vessel lay effecting the relief of the lighthouse crew. Three hours later we passed her again lying to by the Seven Stones lightship. The wind had freshened and gone north, where it stayed for a week or more, and although Brad managed to prepare for supper a noble stew and a stiff duff, he could take no further interest in it himself. On occasions when the weather was boisterous this happened throughout the voyage, with the result that poor Brad lost a stone in weight. It had the effect, too, of making me feel slightly ashamed to be stuffing myself with food, in preparing which the cook had rendered himself unfit to partake. But I never allowed myself to be entirely overcome by these considerate feelings or to suffer my appetite to be impaired by them. Taffy, too, felt no such scruples, besides having an inordinate appetite. As I have said he was powerfully built and had even brought with him a chest expander to increase that power. This miniature Tarzan from the jungles of South Wales needed a lot of nourishment.

Noddy, on the other hand, always passed over breakfast in favour of sleep and spent the rest of the day waiting for supper. At this he did more than his duty before retiring, like a small, sea-going boa-constrictor, to await the passing of another food-less twenty-four hours. Brian Hill was a poor trencherman, too. In fact we saved so much food on this voyage that the necessity of making another to consume what was left over soon became apparent. Brian had another idiosyncrasy. Whatever the weather, sunshine or storm, he never went on deck other than fully equipped in oilskins, seaboots, gloves, and cap of some kind. He put me in mind of a Sherpa we once had with us on Everest who, possibly because he had never before worn anything but homespun wool, wore everything we gave him—windproofs, mittens, Balaclava, boots, snow-glasses—even at base camp in the finest weather, as if a blizzard was imminent.

At about this early stage we first noticed a strange smell in the cabin, all pervasive and difficult to pin down, which I attributed to either a dead rat, fermenting rice, or uncommonly bad cheese. We had on board, stowed in the cabin, six whole ten-lb Cheddars, each in a soldered tin. The smell having become intolerable we got to work with a cold chisel to open up all the cheeses. In three of the tins — and it is still a mystery how it got there—we found an inch or two of water. All was not lost. I housed the three sickly invalids in a box on deck where they could enjoy the sun and the wind. They were the last and by no means the worst to be eaten. Good judges, such as Taffy and myself, spoke highly of them, especially when alleviated with a raw onion.

The north wind blowing straight down the Irish Sea resolved any doubts I may have had about which course to take. We steered west or a little north of it and in the next week logged over 600 miles. So persistently did the wind hang in the north that when ten days out we had not even reached the latitude of Barmouth. Still we were well out in the Atlantic, 300 miles west of Ireland, where it is usually harder to make westing than northing. In spite of this it proved to be a slow passage. In the twenty days it took us to reach the Vestmanaeyjar, south of Iceland, the average run was only sixty-three miles a day and on only four days did we log over 100 miles. On the 13th, with the wind dead aft, we resorted to the twin headsails boomed out from the mast, having this time not forgotten to bring their iron collar. Progress was slow, only thirty-four miles in the day, and while we were reverting to fore and aft rig a ship came in sight. The sail changing seemed to worry those on board her. From a position several miles astern she turned and came back towards us. So we hove to while she ranged close alongside, her engines stopped, to ask if we were all right. She was the *Teneriffa* of the Norwegian Wilhelmsen lines whose ship's names all begin with a 'T'. Her captain offered to report us and we much appreciated their having gone out of their way to speak us.

In making the Vestmannaeyjar, a group of islands twenty miles off the Iceland coast, we intended putting in at Heimaey, the largest and the only inhabited island of the group. Close by is the volcanic island of Surtsey which we had visited the previous year, and just before sailing I had heard that a new island had appeared close by. Accordingly we steered for Surtsey. On the 15th at 9 a.m. we saw a huge column of smoke about thirty miles off. As we drew near we could see that the smoke issued from this island and that Surtsey, about a mile west, was practically dormant. In comparison with its diminutive neighbour which was making all the fuss Surtsey looked enormous. It is now about one and a half miles long, a mile wide, and 600 feet high. Its smooth contours contrast strangely with the steep-sided islands and islets of the Vestmannaeyjar. The new island was in full eruption and we hove to about a half-mile off to watch. The vast white column of smoke and steam ascended continuously while every few minutes an explosion flung a jet-black cloud of smoke and ash, and lumps of pumice hundreds of feet into the air. Away to leeward, below the white smoke, curtains of ash drifted down to the sea. After about an hour we let draw to resume our passage to Heimaey and as we started a plane arrived from Iceland to watch the volcano. Whereupon the eruptions stopped, the smoke ceased, and the unlucky plane, after circling for some time flew home. Surtsey and the new island have enabled a few enterprising people to earn some money. Besides the chartering of planes for interested spectators, coloured picture postcards of the volcanoes in action are sold in large numbers.

With a very fresh beam wind we made about seven knots for most of the twenty miles to Heimaey. To reach the port at the north-west

Among the fishing boats, Heimaey, Westman Islands

Floes and bergs in Sehesteds Fjord

corner of the island we had to pass close under an 800-foot high cliff whence the baffling down draughts and wind eddies obliged us to down sail and motor. To find the way in we had only to follow the numerous small trawlers and drifters, one of which overhauled us close enough to throw on board half a dozen fine haddock. As we turned to open up the narrow harbour entrance, passing between the cliffs and Faxasker, an islet about a quarter mile off, we met a confused sea and a violent wind blowing straight on to those appalling cliffs. The fishing boats, going faster than we were, plunged their bows under amidst sheets of spray. We were reminded of how dependent we were upon our engine at that moment by the sight of the wrecked British trawler *Goodwood* lying under the cliffs just outside the entrance. Her engines, we were told, had failed.

At the first fish quay we passed a small crowd watching us, so we stopped to ask where we could lie. Several English voices directed us to a berth. In Heimaey there are a surprising number of young English, Scots, and Irish who go there to work either in the fish factories or the fishing boats for what seemed to us to be princely wages. Some intended to stay only for the summer, others had been there two or three years. It is the second busiest port in Iceland, devoted entirely to fishing, and the boats that use it—trawlers, herring drifters, seine-netters, ring-netters, or long liners—are all local boats, most of them small. Although they are all Icelandic boats they are supposed to have regard to various fishing limits according to the type of boat. Trawling, for instance is not allowed within six miles of the shore. But they told us that the fishery patrol vessel had a hopeless task. Its movements are passed on from fishing boat to fishing boat, and even the time when the air patrol takes off from Reykjavik is immediately known.

We lay astern of a cluster of fishing boats lying three, four, and five abreast at the quay. We were glad to be in, for it was now blowing a gale and raining. There are two fish-processing factories that work day and night, one of them turning fish and fish offal into fish-meal and fertiliser. We lay downwind of the latter and suffered accordingly, but we could not complain for they allowed us to use their hot showers.

The owners of the fishing boats reputedly make a great deal of money and in Heimaey there are not many ways of spending it. One way is to buy a motor car and this they do in spite of the fact that there are only nine miles of road. Another way, I imagine, is at the cemetery. Nowhere else have I seen such massive and elaborate marble and granite tombstones, some of them, family vaults, constituting a whole wall about twenty yards long. The most avid cinema-goer could not spend much money because there is only the one, and the shops are few and remarkably unattractive. The cemetery happened to lie in my way on a walk up to the volcano, or rather the grass covered crater of a long defunct volcano, for Heimaey, like the other islands of the group, is of volcanic origin. At the crater there was a pillar with an inscribed copper plate pointing to various prominent landmarks, including Hecla on the mainland. On our second day there I took a solitary walk up the very steep, mostly grass-covered rock called Klif, nearly a thousand feet high. In the prevailing gale and driving rain, coupled with the oilskins and the gumboots I was wearing, I rated the climb as 'very severe!' On the summit ridge I came across a rope, formerly used no doubt by those who took the sea birds—auks, fulmars, kittiwakes, and gannets, that haunt the cliffs.

CHAPTER XIX

REYKJAVIK AND ANGMAGSSALIK

◆───────────

T HE SEASON BEING STILL EARLY we decided to go first to Reykjavik where we might be able to get some news about ice conditions. On the 15th we sailed and the next evening passed through the channel between Reykjanes, the south-western extremity of Iceland, and Eldey, a steep rock 226 feet high which is reputedly one of the largest gannet colonies in the world. Even at this distance away streaks of ash and pumice from the new volcano could be seen on the water. Very early in the morning as we lay becalmed about thirty miles from Reyjkavik we were passed by the *Bremen*, a large German cruise ship. Late that evening, as we crept slowly up the buoyed channel into Reykjavik, she passed again outward bound, her tourists having 'done' Iceland.

Reykjavik lies at the back of a fifty-mile wide bay called Faxafloi. It was a warm, pleasant day, clear, the wind light, and we were in no hurry—all conditions conducive to carelessness. Moreover, having been there before, we thought we knew the place. So instead of laying off the course from the chart, I thought I could recognise various features and went bumming on to what on closer inspection proved to be the small fishing port of Keflavik where there is an American air base. Thus, a long way off course, we still had twenty miles to go and did not reach Reykjavik until late evening. Anxious to have supper we made fast at the first fish quay we came to and were busy eating one of Brad's curries when we were told in strong Icelandic to shove off. At the same moment two Customs officers arrived. They were genial enough, spoke good English, and told us where to move to when we had finished supper. The fishing boat to which we finally made fast at a nearby jetty was undergoing repair so that we lay there undisturbed throughout our short stay.

Next morning I went to the harbour offices to clear the ship and pay light dues. The young clerk made out a bill for 400 kroners, a kroner being worth about 2d. I remembered that the previous year we had paid 50 kroners and I resolved that on this occasion, like the hero in Stanley Holloway's *Runcorn Ferry* episode, I would rather be 'drownded than done'. The battle was prolonged. Fortunately the office kept very complete records and when the clerk turned up those for 1964 there it was in black and white: *Mischief*, 50 kroners. I got the impression that unlike the previous year, when we had benefited by the goodwill reflected by the Duke of Edinburgh's visit, we were not popular. None of our former acquaintances, either the drunk or the sober, showed up, and no one gave us any fish. Then it had been, so to speak, British week, now it was very much German week. Besides the *Bremen*, two more German cruise ships arrived to make a long stay, one of them a very modern vessel from Rostock in East Germany.

Thinking that our best bet for obtaining an ice report would be through the American air base at Keflavik I went to the British Embassy to ask for an introduction. The young lady receptionist evidently thought I looked like a Distressed British Seaman waiting for a free passage home, as I suppose I may have done, but even when I had eluded her and reached the Ambassador, whom I knew slightly, I got no change. Keflavik and the American base were seemingly beyond human ken. It occurred to me then that the harbour master at Angmagssalik who had been helpful the previous year in several ways, including the lowering of our stock of whisky, might still be there. So I invested some capital in a reply-paid cable asking whether by the end of July ice conditions would allow of *Mischief* entering the place. Two days later came the laconic reply: 'Should be possible'.

Upon this we decided to sail on July 24th and got busy buying what stores we needed and taking on water. Before leaving I went out to the meteorological office which is housed in the control tower at the airport. Reyjkavik must be one of the few capital cities of the world where the airport is within easy walking distance. The airport is also remarkably free and easy. I merely walked into the control tower and having explained what I wanted was at once made welcome. Two of those on duty in the meteorological office were busy playing chess and the third was free to devote himself to discussing the Greenland ice and weather. What they knew about the ice confirmed the harbour-master's signal—only about 3/10 ice cover in the neighbourhood of Angmagssalik. I was shown all round the control tower and from the roof they pointed out the mast of a twelve-ton ketch, recently bought and sailed over from the Clyde, the first yacht to be based in Icelandic waters. It had been acquired through the combined efforts of forty members of a newly formed yacht club who deemed it shameful that a seafaring nation such as Iceland should be unrepresented in the yachting world.

From Reykjavik to Angmagssalik across Denmark Strait is about 400 miles and seven days elapsed before we sighted Greenland's mountains. The summer in Iceland had been exceptionally fine and the first two or three of these seven days were quite flawless provided one did not mind standing still. For a whole day, the sea like a mirror and the sun hot, we lay on deck watching the snow-capped Snaefell (4000 feet) some sixty miles away. I had my last bucket bath, the sea being still comparatively warm at 50 °F. We saw several whales, schools of porpoise, and small flocks of fulmars always gathered round the boat when she lay becalmed. When over a hundred miles from Iceland we picked up a 'dan' buoy that had broken adrift. The two stout twelve-foot bamboo poles were floated by means of nine metal floats like small footballs roped together in a net, and were kept upright by a length of heavy chain. When we began hauling in the rope we thought it would never end and finally finished up with a 300-foot coil of good two inch manila. One of the bamboo poles from this useful find came in handy later on.

On the evening of the 29th in Lat. 65°30′ Long. 29°50′, when we happened to be steering in that direction, I thought I could see ice 'blink' to the north, a characteristic yellowish tinge in the sky which often denotes the presence of ice below. It seemed improbable, for we were nearly 200 miles east of Angmagssalik, but at midnight I was called on deck. Sure enought ice lay ahead. At first I took it to be a stray raft of floes or a mass of bergy bits left by the collapse of an iceberg. On climbing the shrouds, however, I could see ice stretching away interminably to the north-east. The sea temperature near this pack-ice was 39° F. and an hour later, having gone about and steered south, we found it to be 52°. The presence of an iceberg has no effect on the sea temperature; as might be expected, the presence of pack-ice has a very marked effect.

Angmagssalik, in Lat. 65° 40′, is a little north of Reykjavik, in Lat. 64°10′. Some fifteen miles east of Angmagssalik and slightly north of it is Cape Dan, marking an abrupt bend of the coast to the west and forming a sort of bight at the back of which lies Angmagssalik. The south-going East Greenland current extends to about fifty miles off the coast and, as I had an exaggerated notion of its strength, I made the mistake of aiming for the coast north of Cape Dan, a neighbour-hood where ice notoriously accumulates. On the 30th with a bitter north-east wind, overcast, and some patches of fog and sea-smoke, we got no sights. At midnight, when it was still quite light, the fog cleared revealing a magnificent stretch of wild, mountainous coast about forty miles away. No ice anywhere in sight, not even a berg. The day remained wonderfully fine and by evening when we had closed the land, we had many bergs in sight and could hear the ominous growl-ing of the pack-ice. In the absence of any wind we let her drift and enjoyed a quiet night.

Motoring west in the morning we soon met the pack. Encouraged, perhaps, by the harbour master's signal we thought to try conclu-sions with it but we had not to penetrate far before prudence advised a retreat. All day we drifted, sailed, and occasionally motored south with the ice edge close to starboard until, by evening, the ice forced us to steer east of south. Rather than waste fuel we stopped and let her drift with the current. We reckoned we were about twenty miles east of Cape Dan with ice all in between. It was another perfect evening, not a breath of wind, no ripple on the water, only a gentle swell. As the sun dipped briefly behind the jagged peaks, now a deep indigo, the open water between us and the ice edge assumed a coppery sheen, and as each swell passed and the back of the swell lost the evening light, the coppery sea became streaked with bands of steel.

The following day was just as perfect as with a light south-west breeze we stood away from the coast on a long board until, towards evening, we turned once more in the direction of the land. At midnight, sailing slowly, we had a glimpse of ice to the north but we appeared to have rounded the bulge, for by morning we had open water in sight everywhere. According to my dead reckoning Cape Dan now lay about twenty miles to the north-west. It is the one mark on the coast that can be recognised for it has on it a great radar reflector globe, part of the Distant Early Warning System. I took three sights all of which put us twenty miles further west. I refused to believe them, attributing these odd results to mirage of which we had had some notable examples. We had noted with astonishment the previous morning the ice edge, about a mile distant, looking like an ice cliff 100 feet high. So we held on steering northwest and wondering what the devil had happened to Cape Dan, searching with binoculars all along the coast ahead, until at 11 a.m. Noddy suddenly spotted the great globe about ten miles to the *north-east*.

It is embarrassing for the navigator when making his final approach to have to order an alteration of course of nearly eight points. One cannot claim that the target has moved or is moving. How stupid is it possible to be if after so many voyages I could believe even doubtful sun sights to be less trustworthy than dead reckoning? We met no ice at all until near Angmagssalik when we had about five miles of scattered floes to traverse. I appreciated then the mistake we had made in closing the land too far north. Had we approached Angmagssalik from the south-east we should have seen no pack-ice and saved two days.

On the afternoon of August 3rd we anchored in our old berth outside the small harbour with a warp to a holdfast on the rock shore twenty yards away. From the harbour master, who soon paid us a visit, we learnt that the ice had been very heavy up to about July 15th when it began clearing rapidly. The old *Ardvark*, a wooden Norwegian vessel, had been caught in the ice and spent a month in it drifting south. She is chartered for the summer and seems to spend most of her time fetching sand for cement work from a neighbouring fjord. The new three-storey warehouse on the quay that had been begun last year was well advanced. Later our old friend the *Ejnar Mikkelsen* came in and her skipper Niels Underborg came on board. The previous autumn he had taken her to Denmark for repairs and to the dismay of the Greenlander crew, who were not used to the open sea, they had had a rough passage.

We collected our mail, had showers, and allowed the Greenlander women to put our clothes through the washing machine. Martin, the Danish shipwright-carpenter, rowed over to see if we were still leaking, and when the harbour master came for his evening peg he brought two beautiful white loaves baked by his wife. We learnt that a plane was due in with mail on August 6th so we arranged with the harbour master to go alongside the quay on that day for oil and water. Mail is brought from Sondre Stromfjord in West Greenland and the plane lands at Kulusuk near Cape Dan where there is an air strip. On the afternoon of the 6th, *Ejnar Mikkelsen* duly came in with the mail from Kulusuk and an hour later we were on our way. On the previous voyage we had spent three weeks in Angmagssalik more or less ice-bound; this time we spent only three days.

During our short stay I had gone twice up Spy-glass Hill, partly for old time's sake and partly to look at the ice. What I saw of the ice had led me to suspect that we might have more trouble in getting out than we had had coming in, and so it proved. Once outside King Oscar's Havn we met a strong southerly wind. Even motoring close in to the shore we made little headway and I decided to sail through the belt of ice floes and out to sea where we could make some use of the wind. With the wind abeam we were soon among the floes, with the wind moderating. We continued under sail and since the wind became less and less we started the engine to help the sails. This was a mistake. We ran foul of a floe and the wind in the sails, light though it was, prevented us from getting clear. By this time fog had come down and the floes proved to be much closer packed than those we had come through a few days before.

When manoeuvring in ice it is very easy to run against a floe or to get oneself boxed in. It is a case of he who hesitates is lost. Enough way must be kept on for making quick turns and one must decide quickly which way to turn—especially when visibility is restricted as it was then, when we could not see where open water lay, and where what looked like a promising lead either became too narrow to turn in or ended in a cul-de-sac. Steering by compass as near east as we could, ignorant as to whether that was our best course, and becoming more and more frustrated, at last at ten o'clock we saw the open sea about a hundred yards away. The floes at the ice edge were tossing violently in the swell and we passed them with the utmost caution. We hoisted sail again and headed south-east.

The passage of 180 miles to Skjoldungen proved to be as troublesome as it was short. Fog and light winds persisted all the next day and similarly on the 8th except that the fog was denser and wetter. We heard two ships close by, hooting, presumably, at each other and not at us, and we were relieved when the sounds gradually drew away. There are no fishing banks off that coast and we wondered what these two ships were and whither bound. In the evening, the weather as thick as ever, I was startled by the helmsman's report of 'Land on the port bow', the nearest land in that direction being Iceland. It proved to be a large iceberg about a hundred yards off and since we were making a lot of leeway we missed it by less than I liked.

A brief clearing next morning showed the coast about fifteen miles off and the incessant grumbling of the pack-ice warned us that we were too near. There were over-many bergs about, too, for comfort, so that when a fresh north-westerly breeze sprang up, accompanied by drizzle, we took advantage of it to steer south, a course that would take us steadily away from the coast which trends south-west. We had what would have been a day of glorious sailing had it not been so cold and wet. We did five knots most of the time and during my watch I scored an extremely near miss on a whale. He surfaced less than twenty yards ahead and *Mischief*'s stem cut across the smooth slick he left as he dived to avoid us. In the evening when I thought we had run our distance we ran west for about twenty miles until having sighted icebergs we hove to for the night. The bergs drift with the current and the majority of them are generally within twenty miles of the land. At night at this time there were several hours of darkness.

In the morning we let draw and started to close the land in good visibility but a completely overcast sky. I badly needed a sun sight, preferably a noon sight to give us our latitude. We had not much idea where we were and still less about how to recognise Skjoldungen. The mass of jagged peaks ahead meant nothing to us who had nothing by which to identify them. It is hard to identify any part of the Greenland coast. The innumerable islands that fringe it all look much alike while few of the capes are unmistakably prominent. Fjords occur every few miles so that it is easy enough to enter the wrong one. All depended upon our seeing the sun and the sky remained obstinately and heavily overcast. But luck was with us. Just before noon a wan sun showed faintly through the cloud and we found we were about five miles south of the fjord entrance. There was little ice about and it now became a simple matter to recognise and reconcile the islands and capes shown on the chart with those on the ground. That evening we found a good anchorage ten miles up the fjord.

CHAPTER XX

SKJOLDUNGEN AND HOMEWARDS

———◆———

W E HAD LEARNT AT ANGMAGSSALIK that the settlement at Skjoldungen where, besides Greenlanders, there was a Greenland Trading Company store, was about to be removed. One reason given to us
was that the natives had taken to brewing some kind of hooch from
sugar; another, that owing to the few seals there they could no longer
support themselves by hunting. Anyhow they were being moved to the
Angmagssalik district and when we passed the settlement that evening
there were obviously only a few Greenlanders left. By September 15th,
we were told, all would have gone, and Skjoldungen Fjord would be
deserted. There were the usual painted wood huts, quite a number of
them, but I thought it looked a fairly grim spot, stuck under some dark
cliffs. As we passed some children waved to us from the slightly dilapidated huts.

We anchored in a well sheltered bay, fronted by an island, called
Halvdans Fjord, a much more cheerful spot, with plenty of vegetation
on the surrounding shore and a good stream running in. That night
only the rumble of a distant avalanche broke the profound stillness.
South Skjoldungen where we were is about twenty miles long and generally about a mile wide. At its north end it is connected by a narrow,
deep channel with North Skjoldungen, so that the land between the
two fjords, Skjoldungen proper, is an island. Both sides of the fjord
are mountainous and many small, steep, broken glaciers descend to
the water. The peaks vary from 3000 feet to over 6000 feet, are of all
grades of difficulty and all unclimbed.

As we motored up the fjord next morning, and as I scanned the
snow-plastered faces, the stark walls of rock, and the steep, aspiring
ridges that no climbing party had as yet seen, much less attempted, I
began to wonder whether such a weak party as ours had any business
there. Perhaps I had never quite believed we would get there, for only
now did a fact that I had known from the first begin to bother me. Kiwi

had joined with no ice-axe and boots that were not all they might be, and I had done nothing about it. A peak on the north side that I finally decided we might manage seemed about 5000 feet high, too high, I felt, for me to climb from sea level in the day. Its glacier ended about 1500 feet above the sea and could be reached by a steep slope of rock and scree. Two miles short of it we found a small bay where the water was shallow enough for us to anchor. Next day, carrying light loads, four of us set out along the beach, intending to put a camp on the glacier. On rounding the last corner we found that another glacier, hitherto hidden, cut us off from the foot of the rock slope. Its snout entered the water and higher up it was broken by a 500-foot wall of rock down which cascades of snow and blocks of ice were constantly falling from its upper section. Frightening though it was we were out of range of this cannonade, but we had some 400 yards of crevassed, rotten, and steep ice to cross and I decided that we had better not cross it. Three of us had never been on a glacier and two would have to recross later alone. So we ate our lunch and walked back to the boat in increasing wind and rain. A prudent decision that saved Kiwi and me thirty-six hours of discomfort in a wet tent. All that night and throughout the next day it rained hard and blew unceasingly.

Having moved the boat two miles up to beyond this unfriendly glacier four of us toiled up the slope of rock and scree and gained the glacier above—a gently flowing glacier of rough ice almost free from crevasses. For a camp site we appeared to have the choice of the glacier which was at least flat or a chaotic mound of boulders where we should be warmer. Having had some experience in these things I climbed up the mound and soon found a place that with some delving and heaving could be made to hold the tent. None of the boulders or embedded rocks could defeat Taffy once he got his back to them. We soon had the tent up and were able to give the carrying party, Taffy and Brian, a cup of tea before they went down.

We passed a surprisingly warm night and set off across the glacier to the foot of our ridge on a perfect Greenland morning, clear, warm, and still. After some easy climbing on rock and snow we gained the crest of the ridge and could see where it rose steeply to the summit about a thousand feet above. The snow slope leading to the rock summit looked much steeper than I had imagined from below.

I should not have cared to be on it myself without a steadying axe and we should have to descend after the sun had been on it for some time. We would, of course, be roped and although Kiwi was eager to try I did not think it good enough. There is a disadvantage about my plan of sailing to remote regions in order to climb, especially in the circumstances in which I am often placed, as I was then. At the back of my mind there is always the thought that any mishap on the mountain would also involve *Mischief* and the crew in great difficulty. This, perhaps, made for over-cautiousness. As Dr Johnson said: 'Prudence quenches that ardour of enterprise, by which everything is done that can claim praise or admiration, and represses that generous temerity which often fails and often succeeds.'

That hot, sweltering afternoon we carried the camp down. The glacier stream entered the fjord near where *Mischief* lay in a series of cascades, and while waiting for the dinghy to take us off Kiwi and I sat under one of these to wash off the grime and sweat of a long hot day. The sun had brought out the mosquitoes in force. On board they were less troublesome than on shore where they drove one quite frantic, and at night on watch (which we always kept) they ceased to trouble us. My watch that night passed quickly. The night was dark and the sky clear and I watched the northern lights weave strange patterns of scintillating colour. The putter of a motor boat came from across the fjord and I signalled what I hoped was the Eskimo equivalent for 'What ship?' She came alongside, two men on deck and two asleep below. I shone the torch over her hopefully, expecting to see some salmon—there is a salmon river at the head of Skjoldungen—but all I saw was one huge seal and a small one, the latter half-skinned. I gave them some cigarettes and they chugged off for the settlement.

Re-entering Halvdan anchorage I realised we had a peak on our doorstep, a peak of about 3000 feet that could be climbed from the boat, that looked both interesting and within our limited abilities. A glacier covered with hard snow took us to a col at about 2500 feet whence moderately steep rock led to the summit. At only one point, where we had to cut a few steps across a patch of ice, did we have to use the rope. Having lunched and built a cairn we started down by a different route and, after many false casts down gullies that ended in cliffs, contrived to get ourselves lost. Ultimately we reached a valley on the wrong side of the mountain where we enjoyed a brief and icy bathe. It had been a brilliant, hot day, we ourselves were tired, hot, and sweaty, so that this refreshing dip in a Greenland tarn certainly merited inclusion in my list of memorable bathes. Walking back along the shore of Halvdan we came upon a motor boat from the settlement with a party of youngsters gathering bilberries and bathing in the fjord. I had always imagined that Eskimos were averse to water but here they were larking and swimming in the icy water as if it were a South Seas lagoon. On reaching the boat we discovered that our own brave efforts in the tarn, or even those of the Greenlanders, did not rate very highly, for Taffy had just swum from the boat to the island, a distance of about 300 yards. True, he had taken the precaution of being accompanied by Brad in the dinghy and when we returned he was still a little purple.

One of the most shapely of the Skjoldungen peaks lay on the south side opposite to Halvdan Fjord. It had taken my eye immediately upon our entering Skjoldungen but I did not think it was within our grasp. In order to have a closer look we crossed the fjord and anchored off a very large glacier which stopped short of the water by a quarter mile. Although the surroundings were grim the anchorage was excellent, the water shoaling gradually and there was good holding ground. On a grey, misty day, Taffy, Noddy, and I walked over the rough ice of the glacier for about five miles to see if this peak had any easier ridge than those we had seen. In such matters the weather may affect one's judgement. On a sunny day this peak might have appeared to me less daunting than it did then as I sat caressed by an uncommonly cool wind while wisps of mist writhed round its distant summit. For that time anyway its challenge was to remain unanswered.

So much for Skjoldungen where, had we arrived the previous year, when I had with me a comparatively strong party, we might have attempted some worthwhile peak. Before leaving for home I wanted to have a look at Sehesteds Fjord, the next fjord to the south. We had first to water the ship, preferably at a stream that did not flow direct from a glacier. We headed for the narrow entrance of a small bay nearby where a likely looking stream entered. The first cast of the lead gave 'no bottom at ten fathoms, and the next 'one fathom'. As *Mischief* draws seven feet we were obviously aground but we had gone on so gently that we hardly noticed it. Nevertheless with the engine 'full

Looking up Skjoldungen Fjord

Iceberg, 'picturesque' type

astern' she refused to move. We lost no time in running a kedge out astern and bringing the warp forward to the anchor winch. With the combined power of the winch and engine she came off so fast that we had not time to stop the engine before the warp had taken a turn round the propeller shaft. With no sails up, the engine useless, and the rocky shore close at hand, we hastily dropped the big anchor which fortunately took hold.

So there we were in deep water with the sixty-lb CQR anchor dangling from the propeller shaft on a three-inch warp. After about an hour of patient grappling, arms and shoulders under water most of the time, Taffy managed to get hold of the warp below the propeller and we got the anchor on board. The bamboo pole, a product of the 'dan' buoy incident, now came in useful. After securing a knife to it with Jubilee clips we sawed away at the warp where it went round the shaft until the free end eventually dropped off and sank. Finally we went back to Halvdan to water at the stream there. Floating the rubber dinghy right into the mouth of the stream we filled it with buckets and towed it back to the ship. Unable to rig a pump we passed the water up in buckets, through the cabin skylight, and so into the main tank under the table.

By then, August 23rd, the coast was free of ice except for bergs but in the entrance and all the way up Sehesteds Fjord big floes and bergs were extremely numerous. They came from a glacier at the head of Sehesteds Fjord which descends direct from the ice cap. On this account, though Sehesteds is a fine, mountainous fjord, it compares unfavourably with Skjoldungen as a place for climbing. The quantity of ice about made anchoring a problem and at 4 p.m. I took advantage of the first little ice-free bay we had seen and anchored on the south side. In the course of a brief walk ashore I was attracted by a peak on the opposite side, so later we got our anchor and set out to look for an anchorage on the north side. In mid-fjord, floes and bergs clustering all round, we met two Danes, armed to the teeth, in a small motor boat. They were on holiday from the weather station at Tingmiarmiut thirty miles to the south and were bound for the Skjoldungen settlement. We slowed down while they came alongside for a 'gam' but I did not ask them on board as we had yet to find our night's anchorage. It was, I think, the feeling that we had been inhospitable, that later induced us to call at Tingmiarmiut. The north shore proved to be steep-to and heavily infested with ice. At length we found a place off a glacier that had long since receded from the shore, where the water was shallow enough, and prepared for an uneasy night fending off floes.

Early in the morning in my watch a large floe drifted in and shoved its projecting shelf of ice right under the keel. I had visions of the floe capsizing and of *Mischief* being catapulted in to the air by the ice underneath. The above-water part of the floe could just be reached with the bamboo pole and I was able to keep shoving the boat clear. Kiwi and I had another cloudless, windless day for our third and last climb. Having reached the summit ridge on good, hard snow we thought the peak was in the bag. But we came to a series of deep gaps in the ridge, the last forcing us to descend 500 feet before we could traverse across and gain the summit. This peak was at the junction of Sehesteds with a branch fjord in which there was far more ice on the surface than water. In fact so congested were the floes that the fjord looked like a continuation of the glacier we could see at its head from which all the ice came. When we got back to the boat in the evening we learnt that she had had to be moved once on account of ice. Several bergs were still menacingly close so in order to avoid being pestered by them during the night we went back to the anchorage on the south side.

The weather station of Tingmiarmiut is on an island at the entrance to a large fjord of the same name. On the chart it looked as if it should be approached from the fjord side but I had learnt from the Danes we met that the best approach was from seaward by a narrow inlet about three miles long. Instead of going back down Sehesteds and out to sea we saved ourselves a few miles by going up the fjord and then cutting south through a narrow channel behind an island. Once at sea we set a course for Tingmiarmiut twenty-five miles down the coast, having enough wind to sail most of the way. The weather was clear. There was a small group of islands close off the entrance to the inlet which appeared narrower and even more uninviting than I had expected, with some rocks showing on one side. The doubts that I felt about this being the right entrance were dispelled when we spotted on one side of it a small concrete beacon.

It is astonishing to see the sort of places into which large icebergs will find their way. At a sharp bend in this narrow passage, its width varying between a cable and half a cable, we found three icebergs lying across it. We might, perhaps, have squeezed through but decided not to try. Instead we anchored there in a tiny bay with an even bigger iceberg close at hand. This monster was almost certainly aground and would not worry us. From the chart the station must be about a mile beyond the bend. We could hear nothing, and see nothing but the rock walls of the channel, so we uttered a few bleats on our foghorn and then had supper, intending to defer our visit till the morning.

Although by morning the three bergs blocking the way had drifted off I thought it better to walk to the station to see first what the anchorage there was like. Accordingly three of us landed and after a quarter of an hour of rough walking came upon the huts. Twelve husky dogs picketed in a line on a bed of winter snow set up a frightful clamour and presently a man appeared. He offered us coffee but the coffee was accompanied by bacon and eggs, smoked eels, and other delicacies. The fact that we had just had our breakfast made no difference to Taffy and Kiwi. The other six men then began to drift in and in due course they took us back to *Mischief* in their launch so that we could bring her up to the anchorage. Before doing this we could not resist visiting the huskies who were quite besides themselves with delight at being fondled and spoken too. We went solemnly down the line having a word with each.

The anchorage at the head of the inlet where the station lies is wider than the channel with room for a ship of several hundred tons. There are two big huts, a wireless hut, and a large store. In the living hut is the kitchen with an oil-fired range, dining room, and a big, comfortable lounge with a small billiards table. The two Land-rovers they have cannot be overworked, for they are mainly used for bringing up stores from the jetty when a ship arrives which happens only twice a year, in July and October. Mail can be received all the year round by having it dropped, but it cannot be sent. We spent a cheerful day with the Danes, a day devoted largely to eating and drinking—a meal of half a chicken each and ice cream in the afternoon and another at night.

When we came ashore for breakfast we brought them some rum and cigarettes and before we left we were taken to their store and told to help ourselves—which, on our behalf, Brad did in an all-embracing way. With three of the Danes on board we then motored down the inlet, dropping them at the entrance where a very unpleasant, confused sea was running. With no wind to steady us we were thrown about all day by a sea that was running in every direction. Frequent tide rips added to the confusion and not until we were twenty miles off the land did the sea calm down.

The fast passage that one always expects to make homewards across the Atlantic seldom happens. On this occasion we logged over 100 miles on only four days, and for the twenty-two days from Tingmiarmiut to the Needles the average run was only seventy miles. An unusual occurrence in the North Atlantic was our being able to run for three consecutive days with twin staysails set without touching a sheet, the wind never varying a point, while we logged 270 miles. Few ships are sighted to the north of the main shipping lanes and those few that we do sight always seem to be Manchester Liners. In Lat. 56° the *Manchester Renown* came close to have a look at us and on the same evening after dark I signalled another ship to ask to be reported. She got our name and duly reported us but my reading of Morse is not very hot and I did not learn her name until we got home when I found we had been reported by the *Manchester Engineer*. We met a strange ship in the way of an extremely dirty Russian trawler with apparently nothing to do beyond having a look at us. She would not respond to signals in any form, lamp, flags, or foghorn.

At length, on the night of September 13th we picked up the Bull light at the corner of Ireland and before dawn next morning, Mizzen Head and the Fastnet lights. On the 16th we were three miles south of the Longships, the wind light at south, so light that by evening we were still eighteen miles south-west of the Lizard. One of the concessions to modernity on board *Mischief* is our wireless receiving set and since entering home waters we had begun listening to the Shipping Forecasts. Most yachtsmen, I suppose, listen to these forecasts. A few, perhaps listen with the reverence that they would have accorded to the living voice of one of the major prophets, never dreaming of quitting their moorings, if only to cross the Solent, until they have learnt what is in store.

That evening we were a little surprised to hear a gale warning for the Channel and most parts of the coast, a deep depression being about to pass over the British Isles with its centre somewhere about

Liverpool. If one picks up a gale warning it is prudent to act on it, especially if, as on this occasion, winds of Force 9 and 10 are mentioned. The wind was still light at south and the glass just beginning to turn down, but while we still had daylight we changed the mainsail and working jib for the trysail and storm jib, leaving the staysail set. Throughout the night we sailed on to the south-east in order to get well away from the land. In the morning, the glass falling steeply and wind about Force 6 or 7 at south, with rain, we continued sailing with the staysail set until the increasing wind obliged us to drop it about noon. That afternoon the sea built up considerably, short, steep, and breaking. In fact the seas seemed to be more vicious at that time than they were later when the gale had fully developed, when the wind blowing at full blast appeared to smooth them out. At 4 p.m., on account of the wind direction and the breaking seas, we hove to on the starboard tack. Had the wind been west instead of south we could, I think, have safely run before it.

That evening the forecast for 'Plymouth' was laconic: 'Gale Force 10 southerly, veering west later.' The wind certainly went on increasing until towards midnight when the glass began to flatten out. Unluckily we were hove to in a busy shipping lane and since our navigation lamps refused to burn with that amount of wind blowing we had some tense moments. Perhaps nowadays no one can make proper oil lamps, but surely a hundred, or even fifty years ago, when oil lamps were in common use at sea, a gale of wind did not promptly blow them all out.

We had our Aldis lamp for emergency use but I dislike flashing it at an oncoming, unsuspecting ship, especially on a stormy night, partly because it might be taken for a call for assistance, and partly for fear of so upsetting the officer on watch that he might give the wrong helm order. I think it best to refrain, like Brer Fox who 'lay low and said nothin' ', unless pretty confident that there is some danger of being hit. But just before dawn of the 18th my judgement was at fault and this policy of masterly inactivity nearly caused a nasty mishap. When at the eleventh hour, so to speak, I switched on the Aldis lamp the chap at the wheel of the oncoming ship certainly reacted with admirable promptness. She passed to windward at short spitting distance while a stream of abuse in English flowed down to us from her bridge.

First anchorage in Sehesteds Fjord

As the day advanced and the wind eased we began sailing and that night in lovely, clear weather we raised the Portland Bill light. Having anchored off Yarmouth for the Customs to clear us we went up Lymington river on the Sunday afternoon and made fast. Two days later we had stripped *Mischief* bare and the crew went their several ways.

Gratifying though it would be I cannot hope that anyone who reads of these voyages will partake of the pleasure of those who made them, or even of the pleasure that I have had in thus reliving them. Possibly the book may be dismissed as a picture of an elderly escapist in full flight. I do not think that label applies. Besides the voyages themselves, representing our feeble challenges to Poseidon, each voyage had a purpose, frivolous though to many the purpose might seem. Rather than escaping from anything we were facing up to reality. As Belloc said: 'Everywhere the sea is a teacher of truth. I am not sure that the best thing I find in sailing is not this salt of reality... There, sailing the sea, we play every part of life: control, direction, effort, fate; and there can we test ourselves and know our state.'

Tilman and Patanela—Outward Bound, 1964

◆

Philip Temple

T HE SKIPPER ARRIVED on 19 October and worked inconspicuously at the rigging and sails, refusing to be rushed into a sailing time until he had the measure of a strange ship and its state of readiness. The food came in truck-loads and amazingly it all fitted 'tween decks. Reluctantly we turned away three-quarters of a consignment of meat pies when 2000 were delivered instead of 500! On the morning of 5 November the Skipper said quietly he thought we were about ready to go. There was hurried last-minute shopping, unwanted gear was piled on the jetty, and we cast off from a crowd of well-wishers at three o'clock in the afternoon. Colin and Grahame had work to conclude and were to join us with Mal in Albany. But we had three able substitutes for the first part of the voyage in Albert Rogers, Jim McCormack and Alex Theakston. We motored away but soon hoisted sail, despite exhortations from the press launch to go faster. A yacht with friends came out to see us off, scraping our side, but soon we were alone, dipping in the swell of the Tasman Sea. Grahame stood above us on the Heads to take photographs as the tiny yellow schooner with new, white sails set out across the untrammelled ocean.

The Skipper never spoke to excess, and when we were on the early watch that morning his opening gambit was very English: 'Not very good weather is it?' A 'moderately rough sea' as he told me to write in the log book. We had a fresh southerly dead ahead so we could not hoist the sails and we pitched and bucked in the short seas with the engine at low revs. At times *Patanela* was awkward to steer at south or south by west as the stern lifted and the wheel spun freely. John and I were with the Skipper on the morning watch and we looked into a white, leery dawn with dirty brown muttonbirds circling and disappearing among the waves. But it was dry to start and only at six did the rain beat down and make life cold and miserable.

There were a few haggard and grey crew members at breakfast. We had not yet been at sea for a day, and frequently above the rumble of the diesel I heard the horrid sound of retching over the rail. Warwick was cook and his rushes to the side while doling out food were not conducive to good digestion. Russ looked ghastly. Gaunt, white, eyes staring glassily at the sea, he sat hunched by the rail in his foul weather suit as Jim twirled the wheel with professional ease and lit a cigarette: 'This is the best cure for seasickness!' Jim had come for the trip round to Albany, our only port of call before the sub-Antarctic. He proved invaluable in those early days when half of us could not tell a peak halyard from a bobstay. He was tall, redheaded, freckled and weatherbeaten from eleven years at sea in fishing boats off his native Tasmania. And he had served with the Beast of Bass Strait: a legendary skipper who preferred a rope's end to a reprimand. Jim's tales of him were hilarious and frequently, if one were steering a few degrees off course, his throaty voice would growl in imitation: 'Don't bother to call the next watch.' Though several would have welcomed missing a watch at that stage, we were all glad to be under way, that the expedition had become a fact and not a project. The apprehensions and worries were still there but now we could come to grips with them. Heard Island seemed lost in time and distance and for those of us who had not sailed before, the biggest challenge was the long voyage in our small ship. All our eggs were in its one basket and there could be no miscalculation that would jeopardise its safety.

Sleeping room for ten men seemed to have been allowed as an afterthought. The Skipper said that it did not matter where anyone slept since all the bunks were 'equally bad'. Allocation of berths was easy. Logically, Warwick slept in the galley next to the stove with the Skipper on the port side, handy to the charthouse and sextant. Both the lockers at their heads and the space beneath their bunks were full of food and Warwick adopted strange bedmates in the form of a mountain pack, kitbag and box full of papers which he insisted would stop him falling out when the ship rolled. There was nowhere else to put them anyway. The smokers were in the fo'c'sle, away from the fuel. That meant John and Ed in the lower bunks, port and starboard respectively, me and Jim, later Grahame, in the top bunks. The bottom bunks had lee boards to prevent us from rolling out but, curiously, not the upper ones. Jim and I did not have far to fall, however, since the deck was buried to a depth of three feet in cartons of bottled beer and cigarettes—a glorious cushion. It was appropriate that the fo'c'sle hatch was permanently labelled in blue paint: *Saloon and Bar.*

Amidships was a wide hold that was normally filled with seawater for keeping freshly caught crayfish. We had cleaned it out, knocked away most of the rust and fitted in bunks made of rough timber above the lower layer of diesel drums. There were two long bunks, about ten and a half feet, so Russ, Antony, Albert and Alex (later Col and Mal) had to suffer an uncomfortable overlap and play midnight footsie until improvements could be made later in the voyage. But here was felt the least motion of any part of the ship, and the cray tank always seemed to remain snug and warm.

Colin wrote and told me in New Zealand that *Patanela* had 'flush decks'. This undoubtedly must be some technical term for, rather than presenting the streamlined aspect of a submarine that I expected, she was as cluttered on deck as she was below. The basic superstructure consisted of a welded deckhouse in keeping with the rest of the ship, an engine-room hatch, a large cowling like a gun turret to cover the cray tank, a deep-freeze hatch and a small cowling to cover the fo'c'sle entrance. But apart from these there were a dozen large cylinders of propane gas for the stove, oxyacetylene cylinders, a cluster of pipes to be used for a radio aerial, a drum of benzine, three eighty-gallon drums for water, a Beaufort life raft for ten men, two store lockers, two pumps, three winches, three air vents, engine exhaust, two escape hatches, anchor winches, anchors, a davit, two barrels of rum and a large tin of biscuits. Add to this the compass binnacle and main steering wheel for'ard of the deckhouse, the full heavy gear of a gaff-rigged schooner, and some other bits of paraphernalia which took several days to identify, and 'flush decks' became something of a joke.

Despite all our efforts we could not cram in enough fuel to feed the
165 h.p. diesel for the round trip. Although we would refuel at Albany
there were at least 4500 miles to cover before we returned there. The
engine would have to serve as auxiliary, except when rounding Australia, and our main motive power lay in the seventeen-ounce terylene
sails. Though she was eleven years old *Patanela* had never been seriously
sailed and had spent most of her life pounding away under engine at
high speed in competitive crayfishing. So even her owners could not tell
us how she would handle under sail. With his raw crew, and no opportunity for working up, the Skipper was in for an interesting time.

Not that this situation was new to him. Although sixty-six years
of age, the Skipper had not begun ocean cruising until 1954. Until
then he had made a series of mountain expeditions that will live for
ever in alpine history: Mount Kenya in 1931, Nanda Devi in 1934–1935,
Mount Everest in 1938. In 1950 he was the first to approach Everest
from the Nepalese aspect and thus paved the way for the successful ascent in 1953. Added to this was service in both World Wars,
the DSO, Military Cross and Bar, and fighting with Albanian parti-
sans in 1944. Later he looked to a fresh challenge and chose to sail
to his mountains. Since 1954 he had covered some 100,000 miles in
his forty-five-foot cutter *Mischief*; circumnavigated South America and
Africa; made four trips to Greenland and the Arctic; and sailed from
England to Kerguelen, 300 miles north-west of Heard Island, in 1960.
On all his trips he had trouble finding an experienced crew with the
time and energy for a long, hard voyage. Raw hands were nothing
new. This time he had the added responsibility of a strange ship, and
a steel ship at that, with 'iron things all over the place'. She was stiff
and unbending compared to *Mischief* and, for him, there were too
many mechanical contrivances on board. Before long the automatic
pilot was banished, the echo sounder looked at askance and a sugges-
tion that we motor and sail at the same time treated as sheer sacrilege.
Clean, pure sailing was the object and there is no doubt that for
unadulterated enjoyment and a comfortable ride the sails had it over
the Rolls-Royce every time. Then the jerky unnatural motion and the
noise would be gone as the ship, clouded in white terylene, dipped
and slipped through the swell to the soft rustle of the sea, with the
occasional flap, thump or creak of blocks.

On 14 November we ran a sweepstake, with Albany beer money as the prize, to see who could make the closest guess of the time we would pass the first 1000-mile mark. As 'entertainments officer' I ran this with great gusto and had to bear the brunt of acrimonious remarks for weeks afterward when I won it myself. At that stage we were about 130 miles south of Investigator Strait and the approaches to Adelaide. On that day, and the days either side, we covered 175 miles and with such good going we expected to reach Albany within a week. The Skipper took the smallest opportunity to raise sail. The slightest favourable wind change and he would have us up on deck, even if it meant that the sails would be up only for an hour or two.

Although some of us felt that this was unreasonable perversity, and a nuisance to be dragged away from a book or pulled from one's bunk, it had the effect of making us work together and gave us practice in time for the rougher days ahead. Though ten of us lived on a small schooner it was not often that we were all together. I wrote in my diary after ten days that we had not shaken down into a very convivial crew and that the discussions we expected to be such a feature of the trip had not materialised. But it had taken time to adjust to a new way of life and the steady strain of keeping watch and catching up on sleep did not contribute towards the formation of a club. 'In some ways this is good since it's going to be longer before we're all sick of each other.' Late one morning, Jim ran down the deck shouting 'All hands and the cook on deck!' as if the ship were on fire and within a couple of minutes there were a number of startled, bleary-eyed men with bare feet and flapping shirts fumbling at ropes as the Skipper gave the order to raise sail. With a mischievous glint in his eye and a slight smile he took the wheel and muttered inaudible imprecations as the main peak was hoisted too soon and a headsail sheet ran out with a rush. But eventually we had the sails up and set, the Skipper brought *Patanela* back on course, and we went back to our sleepy hollows all the better for the exercise and work as a team. An hour or so later the sails were furled again.

The longest day of the year produced a stiff blow from the north-west. We rattled along in fine style under all plain sail, touched six knots before we made our first serious reefing and looked most expert and seamanlike as we lined the main boom in blue foul-weather suits taking in the points. Later the jib had to be lowered as the seas rose. It was a frightening prospect to go out on the bowsprit with no protection as it dipped close to the big waves. But the Skipper set the example, went out himself and grimly pulled down the luff as Russ and Grahame hauled the sail inboard. I was at the wheel and could find nothing but admiration for this incredible man as I eased *Patanela* into the wind. He came off exhilarated, puffing but grinning slightly, a typical, mischievous look in his eye. Life was full of worthwhile challenges—even for a man of sixty-six.

Excerpts from *The Sea and The Snow* by Philip Temple
Cassell Australia, 1966 and Lodestar Books, 2016

H. W. TILMAN

The Collected Edition

FOR THE FIRST TIME SINCE THEIR ORIGINAL APPEARANCE, all fifteen books by H. W. Tilman are being published as single volumes, with all their original photographs, maps and charts. Forewords and afterwords by those who knew him, or who can bring their own experience and knowledge to bear, complement his own understated writing to give us a fuller picture of the man and his achievements. A sixteenth volume is the 1980 biography by J. R. L. Anderson, *High Mountains and Cold Seas*. The books will appear in pairs, one each from his climbing and sailing eras, in order of original publication, at quarterly intervals from September 2015:

www.tilmanbooks.com